Trying
to Be
a
Christian

Trying
to Be

a
Christian

by
W. Norman Pittenger

A Pilgrim Press Book
Philadelphia

Copyright © 1972 United Church Press

Library of Congress Cataloging in Publication Data

Pittenger, William Norman, 1905–
    Trying to be a Christian.

    1. Christian life—Anglican authors. I, Title.
BV4501.2.P555   248'.48'3   72–1567
ISBN 0–8298–0237–1

Contents

1

Where Am I Going
—and Why?

Sometimes, when we meet a friend on the street and notice that he is moving along more rapidly than usual, we wonder where he is going. Or we see someone in an automobile, driving intently and obviously with a purpose; we may say to ourselves, "Where's *he* going in such a hurry?" We take it for granted that most people, most of the time, are going *somewhere*—home, office, school, store, factory, even church. They have a destination in view and they bend their efforts to reach it.

Furthermore, most people would be able to tell you where they are going and also *why* they are going there. If they are on the way home, it is to be with wife and children after a hard day's work. If their destination is the office or factory, they are probably going to work; if it is school, probably they are students who willingly or unwillingly have the purpose of getting an education. And when people are on their way to church, they intend to join their friends and fellow churchmen in the worship of God.

This very common fact, obvious to everybody—human beings on the move, going somewhere, with some sort of purpose, every day of their lives, if they are able to get around at all—is a symbol of a very deep truth about human existence. By his very nature, it seems, man is "on the way" and he is on the way because he is seeking to arrive at a desired goal. Perhaps this truth explains why, in an older day, a book like John Bunyan's *Pilgrim's Progress* had such a great appeal. Bunyan was writing about people who were on a journey and who had a destination; for him the journey was through the affairs of this present world and the destination was a heavenly city where genuine satisfaction and perfect joy might be found. Nowadays people do not often think like that, perhaps. But it remains the case that stories of travel have their appeal and it is certainly true that much of the world's great literature has been written about man as a traveler, one who is on the way and who hopes before too long to arrive at his desired destination.

The one thing that almost every human being does not wish, at least during his active years, is simply to "stay put," as we phrase it; he does not want to be stuck in one place, with no journeys to make. The Irish poet William Butler Yeats speaks of his love for "the pilgrim soul" of a woman he knew. The very word pilgrim takes up Bunyan's theme and the point which Yeats is making in his poem is that, more than the beauty and cleverness of his friend, he was attracted by that quality in her life which made her restless and kept her continually looking and seeking for ways to go, where she could find deeper truth, better satisfaction, and increasing happiness. When we see people like that, almost inevitably we too are attracted.

Now in this book we are going to consider what it means to become a Christian. The key word here is *become*. It suggests movement; it entails getting or going somewhere—and the purpose or goal, the "why," is in the other word "Christian." The Christian, we shall see, is not somebody who has already arrived, so that now he can settle down into an established state and take his ease. The Christian is a man or woman, boy or girl, who is quite literally on the way—in this case "the Way" of which the New Testament speaks for it uses exactly that word to describe the whole business of Christian profession and practice. The first Christians thought of themselves as those who followed the Way—that path of life indicated to them by everything that Jesus Christ said and did and was. They were going along that Way; and their purpose was to become more and more completely Christ's people so that they lived "in him" and he lived "in them." They had a great hope, to be sure. This hope they expressed by speaking of being with their Lord in heaven, yet they never for one moment forgot that here and now, as they walked in the Way, they were also with that Lord who had gone before them and was still their comrade and friend, their savior and lord.

It seems to me unfortunate that so often we have thought about Christian profession as if it were static and fixed. We ask, "What does it mean to be a Christian?", and then we pile up a series of definitions to see just how accurate it would be to call ourselves, or somebody else, by the Christian name. You are supposed to believe this and that, to do this and that, to be this or that; maybe you qualify, maybe you do not. But to talk in that way is to deny the living, dynamic, vital quality of Christian profession, just as it is to overlook the same quality in human existence itself. *Every* man is becoming something or other; he lives with an aim, however dimly grasped, and he moves toward it, however slowly and falteringly. So too a *Christian* is somebody who makes no pretence to have arrived at his goal but who does know that he is moving toward it. He is indeed on the Way; he is going somewhere and he thinks, or rather he is convinced deep down inside him, that he knows why he is going, as well as where. In the familiar words of Paul, "the measure of the stature of the fulness of Christ" is his objective; that is what he is becoming.

The remainder of this book will consider various aspects of this Christian becoming. It will also try to put that becoming in its proper context in a world which is a "becoming" world—not a world where things are settled once and for all, but a world which is on the move, where novelties happen, and where there are risks and dangers as well as joys and satisfactions. This world, like us men in it, is on the way; it too has a goal or purpose, even if that is not always plainly evident to us.

Becoming a Christian today, as in every other day, is from one point of view a simple thing; but we shall see that in our own time there are also some problems which our ancestors in Christian belief did not have to face, although doubtless they had their own kinds of difficulty too. Yet, at the very end, I hope that we shall be able to agree that the basic simplicity of Christian discipleship—walking on the Way pioneered by Christ, as we may put it—is still very real and true. For myself, I think that what it means to become a Christian can be put in one short sentence: A Christian is a man or woman, boy or girl, who in becoming truly human knows himself grounded in Christ, grasped by Christ, and growing up into Christ. But to be able to say *that* with any sincerity and conviction requires that we shall earn the right and privilege, earn them by thinking hard, with utmost honesty, and by giving ourselves in total self-dedication to the Way in which we walk.

To become a Christian today, as in every other day, demands that we commit ourselves to a certain specific faith and that we live and act in a certain specific way. That is why in this book we shall be concerned with two big topics: with what a Christian *believes* and with what a Christian *does*. The two belong together; there is always a reference back and forth, from one to the other. What we believe in our hearts, we must learn to practice in our lives; what we practice in our lives will reflect what we believe in our hearts.

Thus to be a Christian requires us, first of all, to take a stand. We cannot hope to move forward unless we know the goal toward which we aim and the point from which we start. We have a position, a point of reference: we have a "stance," as a golfer would say. This does not suggest that we never move at all, any more than the golfer will remain forever on the putting-green. But there are good reasons for speaking of our specifically Christian stance. The most obvious of them is just this: none of us, however clever we may be, thought up Christianity for himself. It is not our invention; we received it. We were incorporated into this business of becoming Christians when we became members of the Christian fellowship which proclaims a basic faith. In that sense, everybody who calls himself by the Christian name confesses his dependence upon that which has been handed down to him through the long centuries of Christian history; by necessity, he is a "churchman."

Of course to put it that way raises a great many questions, some of which we shall be obliged to examine. But for the present, the reader is asked to take note of the fact that in the New Testament, which must be our guide in such matters, there is absolutely no possibility of being a Christian without belonging to the fellowship or company of other Christians. Paul serves as a good representative here. For him a Christian was, by definition, a "member of the Body of Christ"; he would have rejected violently, being the sort of man he was, the notion that somebody could be a genuine Christian— although of course he could be a good man or a faithful Jew or a responsible Roman citizen—all by himself, in isolation from others who are Christian. For the apostle, a Christian was part of a living fellowship of those who walked in the Way. He himself had been incorporated into that fellowship when he had his shattering experience of conversion on the road to Damascus; others might not have such an overwhelming moment of decision, to be sure, but nonetheless they were participants in the fellowship, however they may have got into it—and the fellowship was not only with one another but also in and with the Lord who had blazed the Way in which they walked.

In John's Gospel and in the letters attributed to the same author, it is taken for granted that those who have accepted Jesus Christ as their Lord have also, and by that very fact, accepted membership in the brotherhood which constituted the little Christian communities in the Greco-Roman world. To see this plainly asserted, one has only to read the first letter of John, where the criticism he makes about certain people who thought of themselves as Christian is precisely in their having left the fellowship. And for a third and last example, consider the first letter of Peter, where Christians are defined as "living stones" in the great Temple which is Christ himself; they are members of a "royal people," sharing together in the life of their risen King, Jesus Christ. They are participant in a "new" relationship between God and men through Christ; and they have become that through the rite of baptism, with which the letter is primarily concerned. They *belong;* that is why they walk in the way in which they do.

I have said that there are problems here for many of us today. The institutional churches seem much more a fact of sociological significance than a deeply religious reality committed to "turning the world upside down," as they said of the Christian fellowship in the first century. Critics of churches call them stodgy, conventional, unimaginative, out-of-date. The criticism strikes home; there is far too much truth in it for us to deny it or try to evade it. Yet in a way the criticism misses the point. Even if we grant that much of what it says is true, we are still left with the simple fact that nobody *can* be a Christian in separation from his brethren. To be a Christian *means* and *involves* being in closest association with others who accept Jesus Christ as their Lord and who are trying, with whatever degree of success or failure, to become Christian people. If the institutional churches often seem obstacles to faith and provide less than adequate guidance for Christian living, what is needed is not their rejection but their reformation. It has always been that way; which is why there have been, from time to time, great movements for reform in the Christian fellowship and why we must say of the church of Christ as a whole what the great reformers of the sixteenth century used to say: *ecclesia reformata et semper reformanda* ("the church reformed and always to be reformed").

William Temple, one of the notable Christian leaders in the period between the two world wars, said in one of his books: "Let the Church *be* the Church." Perhaps he *should* have said, "Let the Church always *become* the Church"; but anyway that was the point he was intending to make. That is, he was urging that our great necessity is to see to it that the institutional embodiment of the Christian fellowship is always moving toward fuller realization of its purpose and significance: to be the Body of Christ, the instrument in which through many human lives Christ works in the world. The churches which we know are to be judged by the degree to which they seek to become that, to act like that, to teach and live like that, to worship and pray and work and serve like that.

Some critics tell us that the day is now far too late for such a revival or reformation. I do not believe this for a moment. Only in moments of faithless despair could anybody talk in that fashion, forgetting that (if Christianity is true at all) the Spirit of God is at work in the fellowship to bring about, in due time, the revival of life and enthusiasm, loyalty and labor. And in any event, many who make such a criticism themselves look back to the earliest days of Christianity as reflected in the New Testament literature, and judge the contemporary churches by that standard. In that case, they are implicitly recognizing that whatever may be wrong with the present-day embodiment of Christianity in our churches, at its very beginning Christianity *was* a fellowship of which every Christian was a member. Thus they grant the main point we are trying to make; and they goad us, by their very attack, to work and pray for the reform which they despair of seeing. There are enough signs of renewed vitality and dedicated action, in every part of the Christian world today, to give us encouragement—all the way from the steadfastness of Christian disciples under persecution in some parts of the world to the deep concern of others for social and racial justice, not to mention the remarkable work now being done in thinking through, once again, the significance of Christian faith in terms of modern thought and knowledge.

But my readers, like me, are not ecclesiastical leaders or statesmen; we are men and women trying to become Christians in today's world. Hence our present concern is not to seek to work out, even if some of us have the knowledge and skill, the ways in which revival or reformation will take place. We rejoice when we see it happening; we are grateful for the wonderful surge of new life and the deepened understanding of Christian responsibility wherever we see it—in Protestant and Catholic circles and in so many different parts of the world. But *our* concern, here and now, is not with these big issues so much as with our own discipleship. We want to see what it means *for us* "little people," as we might put it, to become Christians—members of the church of Christ, with all its admittedly tragic imperfections and yet with its glorious possibilities, who are dedicated to the attempt to express in our daily living what was said at our baptism to be our Christian vocation: "to be faithful soldiers and servants of Christ, to our life's end."

So we may now return to what I have called the Christian stance, the position from which we start and the goal toward which we aim. What are we talking about when we use phrases like these?

A way of getting at the point is by considering the experience of travel in a foreign country. When an American visits Italy, for example, he finds that in some respects things are as they were at home. If he happens to know a little Italian, he can converse with the natives, share to some degree in their ideas and opinions, and enter into at least a little of their experience of life. Yet he is not really "at home," as we say. He is an American who naturally looks at things from an American point of view. He carries his Americanism with him wherever he goes and it qualifies and conditions everything that he says and does. George Santayana once remarked that an Englishman always takes with him "the climate" of England; so also an American takes with him the fact of his being what he is and the related fact that he is somebody who, being an American, is constantly becoming more an American—and this is true, even if he happens to be critical of his country's policies, dislike some of its characteristics, and perhaps wish that he did not bear the name American at all.

This fact is very obvious when an American visits Great Britain. George Bernard Shaw said that the United States and England are two countries "divided by a common language"; and the American visitor feels this strongly, for their whole cultural background is different, even if related to a common source in early Anglo-Saxon history. An Englishman remains an Englishman when he visits the United States; an American remains an American when he is in England. And when the American returns home after his travels, he feels somehow that he *is* "at home" in a very profound sense, as he could never be elsewhere. This is much more the case when an American has lived for some time in a foreign land where the language is *not* English. Recently an American who has lived in Rome for fifteen years said in an article in a Rome newspaper that he found, on a recent trip back home (his first for a decade), that he had not become an Italian, as he had thought; he *was* an American and nothing could change the fact, no matter how many years he lived abroad.

The explanation here, I suggest, is found in the plain fact that each country naturally and necessarily has developed in its own particular way. Each in its development has created for its people specific attitudes, perspectives, ways of seeing and doing things; and those who have shared in this cultural heritage have inevitably come to reflect those attitudes and perspectives and to see and do things in the way which is appropriate to them. In other words, there is an American stance, as there is a British stance and an Italian stance. So also there is a *Christian* stance.

But the difference is that this Christian stance is not related to this or that place or time. You can be a Christian in Japan or India as well as in the United States or Great Britain or Italy. You can be a Christian in the first century or the sixteenth or the twentieth. It is not the place where, nor the time when, a man happens to live that counts here. His specifically Christian ways of seeing things, doing things, and his attitudes and perspective, his Christian fashion of becoming a man, depend not on time or place but on the stream or current or historical life into which he has been incorporated. The Christian Way has emerged from a long process of historical development. It goes back to the New Testament period and even before that to the Jewish history which prepared for the Christian gospel and life. It has continued down through the centuries to our own day. Anybody who has been caught up in that history and has become a living part of it reflects, to greater or less degree, what the Christian Way historically has shown itself to be. If some scholar reads this book, he will see that what I am here saying is another version of the truth so compellingly stated by Shirley Jackson Case and Charles Clayton Morrison, among others, in the Divinity School of the University of Chicago many years ago.

This Christian history is international, not national; it is potentially world-wide, even if it has been chiefly centered in Europe, the Near East, and North and South America, up until the present time.

Now, since the middle of the last century, it has demonstrated its capacity to include people of every nation, race, language, and social background. You can become a Christian anywhere and everywhere; this is one of the great new facts of our Christian awareness.

At the same time, the Christian stance depends upon one crucial event, or series of events, which took place in Palestine nearly two thousand years ago. Nobody can become a Christian, a human being with Christian attitudes and perspective, without relationship to that event or series of events. We name the event Jesus Christ—and apart from it, the Christian way of becoming would make no sense at all. This is what is really intended when scholars tell us that Christianity, above all other faiths, is *historical;* it has its deep roots in the past and it is conveyed to us today through a continuing community or fellowship of men and women who have accepted and handed on the conviction that this initiating event, Jesus Christ, is in some special fashion both central and crucial. An acquaintance once put this very simply when he said that to be a Christian is, in one sense, to have no faith of one's own, but to make one's own a faith which is received from the whole of our Christian history, and *then,* having done that, to let oneself grow and develop in terms of what has been received.

Now how should we characterize this Christian stance?

I have spoken of specific attitudes and perspectives, ways of doing and seeing things; and this notion helps us to find an answer to the question just raised. The Christian stance, then, is a certain way of seeing and doing things which has its origin in and finds its support from certain attitudes and perspectives. To hold the Christian faith *is* to look at things in this way, sharing that looking with the age-old tradition of which we are part. The attitude and perspective are given in what Alfred North Whitehead, the Anglo-American thinker who died in 1947, once called "the brief Galilean vision." By this he meant the disclosure in Jesus Christ of the way things really go in the world—in other words, the activity of God manifested in what he is believed to have done in and by the life of a man who lived a genuinely human and historical existence at a certain time and place. Here we have the determining quality of Christianity as a stance; here we have also the determining expression of what it means to become a Christian, walking in the Way opened up in the life of Jesus of Nazareth.

There are two characteristics which need to be stressed. One of them is a deep sense of the meaning given to the mystery of human existence. The other is an equally deep sense that everything in the world, including ourselves, is getting somewhere—is on the move toward a goal or purpose which can be shared by the whole creation. The meaning of the mystery was once beautifully phrased by Thornton Wilder in the conclusion of his novel *The Bridge of San Luis Rey:* "Love is the only survival, the only meaning." That is how a Christian sees things. The goal or purpose is that same love which is the meaning in the mystery of our existence, but now it is emphasized that such love is dynamic, active, living, and potent. One sentence might put both sides together: The point of everything is in growing toward the moving forward in love, toward the widest and fullest possible sharing together in a life whose central and dominant motif is nothing other than God, known as the cosmic Love which cannot fail.

Thus the clue to our Christian becoming is to be found in an attitude or perspective which builds on the conviction that whatever surface appearances may seem to be, the mystery of human life *means love;* and that whatever may be the risks, the dangers, the difficulties, in the way, the purpose of human existence and the purpose of the whole universe is to make such love more really visible, more fully realizable, and more adequately expressed. For us men, this carries with it the obvious corollary that our way of doing this is to become more and more genuine *lovers,* in the deepest meaning we are able to give that term. Later on we shall need to unpack what has just been said; for the present, we need only insist that this Christian definition be looked at honestly and bravely.

A Christian is a person of any race or class or nation who looks at the world as a place where love is at work and where Love (the capital letter here indicates that we are talking about God, the supremely worshipful reality in the cosmos) ceaselessly strives to bring about more good to more people in more places and in more ways. God himself *is* Love, as John writes in his first letter; he is "the Love that moves the sun and the other stars," in Dante's words at the end of *The Divine Comedy.* The world in which we live is the place where we can learn what love is and what love gives and demands. The process of becoming a Christian is growing up into that love and thus finding oneself, along with one's human brethren, in love with Love—by which we mean that as a man lives in love with his fellows he discovers, sometimes vaguely and by intimation, sometimes vividly and by conscious experience, that it is "Love that makes the world go round," as the old song puts it, and that this Love is nothing other than the God who creates and saves, suffers and cares, enriches and restores his human children. So we are able to become that which we are meant to become: lovers, however frustrated and broken we may be in our loving. God knows that we *are* frustrated and broken, that our loving can become self-centered and demanding of immediate response, and that we are inhibited, frustrated, disoriented, impotent in our loving. But despite all that, the Christian stance which guarantees the possibility of Christian "becoming" is a conviction that the world is moving toward love, love-in-action and love shared with all creation, a reign or realm of love which the New Testament calls, in its own idiom, "the kingdom of God." In consequence of his taking this attitude and sharing this perspective, a Christian is a man who in his seeking and his doing—imperfectly, inadequately, deficiently, often wrongly—tries to make real in his own becoming human the glorious possibility of such love.

There can be no doubt that a good deal of what is said and done in institutional Christian circles seems inconsistent with what has just been said. People have had and still do have ideas of God which do not stress that "his nature and his name," as Wesley put it, is nothing other than Love. People who call themselves Christians have tended to look on the world as a place to be exploited for their own benefit or as a "darkling plain, where ignorant armies clash by night." People have regarded themselves as hopelessly irredeemable sinners, "worms" who matter to nobody or nothing. And people have seen the world's future as very dim indeed, running down into meaningless stupidity as "a tale, told by an idiot, signifying nothing." *Of course* people have thought that way; some of them have been Christian people, in name at least. To fail to acknowledge this would be blindness or dishonesty. Yet to let that fact hide from us the shining truth that authentic Christianity, historically handed on to us through the great tradition which is the Christian fellowship, proclaims this reality of Love as God, would be to fall victim to a similar blindness and dishonesty.

In this book we are trying to think through the implications of this Christian stance, especially as it affects our growth in our profession —our becoming the Christian people we are meant to become. We cannot forget that no responsible Christian has ever thought that human beings are perfect; our lack of vision is as real as our failure in action. What counts, however, is what we *intend*, with all our hearts and souls and minds and strength. God sees and appraises us in terms of those intentions, although they must be deep and real intentions and not just verbal and superficial ones. If we begin to understand what we are about in becoming Christian, wanting and trying to become Christian in today's world, that deep intention will express itself in a ceaseless effort also to understand and to make actual the stance about which we have been speaking. When we do that, we are at least *beginning* to get somewhere.

When critics, within or outside the churches, say that "the church" has not done this or that, they sometimes talk as if "the church" were a sort of over-all affair which existed entirely apart from the people who make it up. A distinguished church executive once lamented the fact that the frightening economic, racial, and social conflicts of our time did not deeply concern "the church." As I heard him say this, I wondered what he could mean. Did he mean that church assemblies, councils, conventions, conferences, and the like did not often enough speak out clearly on these matters? Probably he did. But he talked as if "the church" meant something which could stand up and act, all of and by itself. Yet the truth is that "the church"—and the universal church, the totality of Christians in the world—means *you and me*, it means that church executive himself who certainly had spoken clearly and compellingly on these issues. The point is that Christian people, knit together in a fellowship of which Jesus Christ is head and lord, *are* what we are talking about when we say "the church" and when we talk about "the churches."

If Christian people, who are those intent on becoming what they profess to be, will grasp more seriously the significance of what we have called the Christian stance, and if they will then set about working it out in practice, each for himself and each in association with others who also seek to become Christians, something very real will be accomplished. None of us can be an *individualistic* Christian, since the very fact of our Christian belonging makes us participant with others; but all of us are *persons*, which is to say that we live together, sharing in a common life, influenced and influencing by our participation with others and enabled in this way to become richer and more loyal in our Christian profession. If the Christian fellowship as a whole is to make its proper impact on the world, it can only be by each of us who "does his thing" as best he can. Each must help others; others must help each one. For this reason, our personal decision to dedicate ourselves to this Christian reality and strive to become the Christians we profess ourselves to be, with our personal growth in understanding and our personal commitment to work, is absolutely crucial.

A famous Victorian scientist and essayist, Thomas Huxley, who called himself an "agnostic" (and in fact invented that word to describe his position), once said that "it does not take much of a man to be a Christian, but it does take all of him." He intended that in a condemnatory way; but how right he was! None of us amounts to very much, as we are prepared to admit in rare moments of absolute honesty. But the possibility of giving all of ourselves to the enterprise of Love in action in the world is still there. Ultimately, that is the thing that matters most. Do we accept what here has been styled the Christian stance? And do we bend our efforts to become Christian men and women, informed by this conviction about Love as meaning and goal, and intent to act, wherever we may be and whatever may be our opportunity, so that such Love may prevail in this tragic yet glorious world where we have been placed for our short span of years?

2

This Worldly World

Anybody who intends to become a Christian must do this at a particular time and in a particular place. It is impossible to be a Christian in an abstract sense, just as it is impossible to be a man in an abstract sense. Each of us lives in a here and a now, a somewhere and a "somewhen." And a man or woman who claims the Christian name and seeks to walk in the Christian Way must undertake these things where he is. The adoption of the Christian stance is made by people who share in the real world in just that place and at just that time in which they find themselves simply by the fact that they are human beings.

If this is true, then it follows that a Christian needs to be aware of the world as it exists in his own time and place. His Christian profession and his Christian discipleship must be worked out under the conditions which that world presents to him. Furthermore, he is naturally open to the many influences and pressures which the world makes upon him. It is impossible to attempt to extricate oneself from the situation; it is absurd even to think of doing this. We live where we are; we cannot be anything other than the twentieth-century people we are, with recognition of all that this signifies. That is why it is not only appropriate but necessary for us to look at this contemporary world and try to see what it is like.

This chapter has been headed "the worldly world"; and the heading has been chosen because it indicates something which we cannot overlook. We might have spoken of a "secularized" world; that would have meant the same thing. However, the words "secular," "secularized," and "secularization" have been overworked in recent years; what is more, they are ambiguous words. "Secular" can mean merely this-worldly or it can mean antireligious or nonreligious. "Secularism" can suggest to us a pattern of life in which God plays no part whatsoever or it can suggest the requirement that everybody pay attention to *this* world and its concerns, whatever he may also wish to say about the divine reality we call God. "Secularization" can mean either the movement in human history by virtue of which more and more people are being forced to reckon seriously with the affairs of this world and assume real responsibility for them, or it can mean increasing disregard for God's purpose and plan in this world. These are but a few of the possibilities; and it is simpler just to say that ours is a "worldly world," in which the interests, demands, and opportunities given in human existence in a finite and limited creation must receive the most serious attention.

I have another reason, too, for wishing to use this adjective worldly. In a significant essay, published some years ago, Alec Vidler used that word as an adjective to modify the noun holiness; he spoke of "worldly holiness," by which he intended a way of becoming a Christian that took much more account than has hitherto been the case of the patent fact that in our own day we need to be aware of the responsibilities and challenges of this present existence, in this present world—he urged that this is precisely what God wants his children to do, now that they have reached the age of relative maturity. In this respect he was echoing the now celebrated remark of the German martyr-theologian Dietrich Bonhoeffer, who wrote from prison to a friend that "man has come of age" and must act like the man he is.

This should not be misunderstood. Dr. Vidler did not pretend that such relative maturity implies that man is entirely adult and can claim complete independence of his Creator. Neither did Bonhoeffer. Both of them were trying to tell us that in the long course of human development the point has now been reached in which we are to consider ourselves responsible for what we do, rather than seek to transfer responsibility for human decisions and actions to a paternalistic God who will relieve us of our humanity, our manhood, and deliver us from the requirement that we do in fact assume such responsibility as is properly ours. When Paul tells us that we are God's sons and that we are to become "men in Christ," he is saying much the same thing. God wants to treat us like sons, like real men, not like little babies or irresponsible adolescents. He has put us here; he wants us to make the most of ourselves in the place where he has put us.

So, by speaking of a worldly world, I have indicated what seems to me a chief characteristic of our time and place. In past ages, many felt that the affairs of this world were relatively unimportant. They believed that they were here only to prepare for a destiny in some other realm, some future existence beyond this world, and that what went on in the here and now did not matter so much. This kind of "other-worldliness," as it has been called, could lead to irresponsibility about what goes on in this present existence; often enough, alas, it did precisely that. But nowadays we know very well that we must take with great seriousness "this-worldly" affairs. We may not think that they are *all* that matters but we do think that they matter a great deal.

This may seem so obvious that it hardly needs saying, yet I venture to dwell on it for a moment. Many years ago a distinguished English theologian said that he knew of no greater "apostasy" or treason on the part of Christians than "putting off to another world what we know should be done in this one." He was referring to the way in which some people at that time considered themselves devout and loyal Christians and yet at the same time utterly refused to interest themselves in social and economic conditions and their improvement; he spoke of the people who declined to work for the eradication of poverty and city slums, saying that after this life the poor, underprivileged, and unjustly treated would receive their due recompense. It was not for Christians to disturb the existing social order; God would take care of the proper apportionment of rewards and punishments in his own good time.

That attitude, certainly, was not so widespread as some have thought. Yet there were many Christians who in one way or another did not feel the keen responsibility which nowadays we feel, to act upon their faith in terms of this present world's needs. Surely no Christian who understands the meaning of his discipleship is likely to talk in that way today, even if there are those who follow a strongly "fundamentalist" line and refuse to concern themselves in any radical way with reform. Most of us believe that we have a duty to do what we can, here and now, to remove poverty, eradicate slums, promote justice, secure racial integration and understanding, and bring about increasing cooperation between classes and groups and nations. What is more, the sensitive man today has such interests very much at heart, even if he is not a professing Christian in any sense. The demand for such worldly action comes not only from those who suffer from the lack of justice, but also from those who are convinced that this justice must be given whether it means difficult adjustments or whether it can be achieved with relative ease.

This is but one illustration of the way in which worldly interests, as I have ventured to call them, have been given a definite priority in our thinking and in our acting. Whether some like it or not, nobody today can evade the truth that the provision of the necessities of life for all men, everywhere, is a duty laid upon us. And associated with this is a growing sense of our planetary existence, where each race and nation is called to assist every other race and nation. The developing countries, as they are now known to us, require the support of those lands which already have progressed to the point of relative security. We live together on this planet and what goes on in any one spot, however remote it may seem, has its effect upon what goes on elsewhere. We are all in this thing together; to realize this and act upon it is one of the big facts of our time. Interdependence on such a planetary scale is demanded in the sort of world which is ours, with its intertwining of interests, with the speed of communication, and with the dependence which makes it impossible for any people in any land to be sufficient unto themselves.

Behind this and behind much else in our contemporary experience is another fact. Everywhere we find increasing use of and dependence upon scientific methods and the discoveries made by contemporary science. Nothing has so radically altered the patterns of common life—in our own lands and increasingly in countries which until yesterday were primitive and "uncivilized"—as this scientific way of seeing and doing, with its tremendous results in technological competence. Everything has been affected. Discoveries that seemed abstract and only of interest to specialists have been shown to have astounding practical application. The field of electronic science is one example; another is the study of man's psychology and his functioning as a total organism, thanks to the devoted labor of depth psychologists. A third is the related research into human cybernetics, where techniques once thought to apply only to machines or to lower levels of the animal creation have been used to improve human methods of acquiring, retaining, and using knowledge. A tremendous change has been brought about through sociological investigation regarding the dynamics of human society, while the study of emotional states and their relation to physical health has brought into existence a new and invaluable approach to the care of man, body and soul.

It is a commonplace to say that science has revolutionized our lives. Its technical application has produced everything from computers which can accomplish tasks that men seem unable to perform, to the atomic weapons whose possible use holds us all in terror but whose background in the use of nuclear energy could promise great things for human happiness and growth. These applications of technology may bring the world to complete destruction; or, they may bring untold blessings, relieving men of drudgery, giving new techniques in surgery, developing new remedies for illness, and providing comforts and pleasures that go far beyond the necessities of life. In recent years the discovery of drugs and other means for relieving mental and emotional disorders provides still one more example of this possible advance.

The result of this change has been that we feel increasingly the sense of human responsibility for what goes on in the world, for better or for worse. We know that the materials and devices, as well as the technical competence, can make human existence a better and happier thing; we know also that we have it in our power to damage and destroy to a degree and in a way impossible for men in no earlier age. And a consequence of all this has been that thought of "another world," where the ills of this one will be remedied, has become much less a vital reality. At the same time and as an inevitable corollary, concepts of a divine being remote from the world which he created or acting in it only as a marionette-show producer who pulls strings now and again, seem to become more and more incredible. So also the notion of God as the "final recipient of the buck," to use ex-President Truman's memorable phrase about the American Chief Executive, no longer makes much sense. God cannot be the *only* really responsible agent, to whom *all* good is attributed and on whom *all* evil is blamed, in a world where we know ourselves to be responsible. Nor can we entertain a view of God as a power or being required only as final explanation of things, the "logical" requirement of a created world; such a deity "cuts no ice" and makes no impact upon those who sense themselves as living in a world which is getting somewhere and where their own role is to play a significant and meaningful part in that movement.

If the "old-time religions" still talk in these ways, they have nothing to say to contemporary men and women. Even the common man watches television, listens to the radio, and reads paperback summaries of modern knowledge; in many ways he is knowledgeable as his ancestors were not. He may not be *wiser;* that is another matter. But certainly he knows more about and is more aware of the things of this world; and for him, men are responsible agents in a world which requires their effort. Although from time to time he may make a polite bow to some dimly remembered remote deity, who supposedly "runs the show" from on high, he does not much concern himself with that deity.

In a world where men light their houses by electricity, they cannot believe that illness is caused by demons. That sentence paraphrases a remark once made by the noted German scholar Rudolf Bultmann. We might develop the remark by saying that in a world where people know what they can do and what they should do, the idea of asking some supranatural deity, invoked for the purpose, to do it for them seems both ridiculous and blasphemous. No contemporary advocate or defender of the Christian faith will get very far if he supposes that this situation is going to change. There are few things more certain than that we are here at a point of no return; and those who find this troublesome had better prepare themselves for something worse, since more and more areas of human life, more and more aspects of the world, are coming within the purview of scientifically oriented men who are convinced that they are responsible for what is done in those places.

We have quoted Dietrich Bonhoeffer's insistence that "man has come of age." This sentence demands a little more attention than we have given it so far. Bonhoeffer did not mean by these words that man is completely and entirely mature; as we have noted, he was under no illusions about this. But he did intend to say that a faith which will be meaningful today must recognize that man has reached the time when he knows himself to be a person with responsibility for his world and when he must act upon that knowledge. It is all very well when little children run to their father as soon as things get difficult for them; it is right for them to see him as their last resort. But when they have "come of age" they no longer can do this, nor would any decent father wish them to do so. They must learn to "stand on their own feet" and act in full awareness of their duty.

This is our present human situation—not so new, either, for the New Testament rings with the affirmation that God now treats us "as sons"—as men who are to accept their vocation to be "fellow-workers" with him. If God were but the last resort, to get men out of their difficulties and to provide answers to all their questions, to deliver them from danger and to assure them that "everything will be all right," he would be like a father who refused to permit his children to grow up but always insisted on keeping them in leading-strings. Most of us would consider such a parent to be a poor father. And God pictured after that model would be a bad "god"—indeed we may doubt that such a "god" ever existed, no matter how many people have liked to think of him in that way.

Perhaps this is why in recent years certain thinkers brought up in the Christian tradition have been led to say that "God is dead." What they are really saying, although some of them would deny this, is that the concept or picture of God with which they have been familiar "has gone dead on them." But that is only to be expected, since so often God has been taken as so remote from his world or alternatively so much an interfering meddler within it as he intrudes from outside, that the freedom and responsibility of men has been called in question or God has become a highly irrelevant idea. A different, better, and I should claim more Christian picture is possible—to it we shall be turning later. All that we need to note now is that for a great many today, not just for the thinkers mentioned above, there is a sense of the *absence* of God.

One of those thinkers has said that what we find is not so much a "sense of God as absent" as an "absence of the sense of God." Perhaps he is right. But I suggest that the reason for this is that God has been identified with a certain model or picture of him and since human beings experience and think largely in terms of models or pictures (whether these are imaginative or rational concepts) the failure of a particular "symbol" can produce an incapacity to reach any vivid awareness of what the symbol is intended to stand for and convey. Yet it is true that when, in an earlier age, people did not believe in God they probably did have a keen awareness of his "absence"; there was some sense in which, as it has been said, there was a feeling that a well-known friend or relation had inexplicably disappeared. Today, William Hamilton tells us, large numbers know nothing like this; for them, the thought of God simply does not occur to them so that they cannot miss his presence or even feel his absence in any vivid fashion.

However, this "all depends. . . ." If by the use of the word God we are seeking to denote some quite clear and precisely defined "being" who stands over there, against us and confronting us, it is unquestionably true that many do not have awareness of such a "being" or of his absence. If by the word we mean, however, something irreducible in all experience, on occasion merely some feeling that life has significance which it cannot give itself, it may well be—I myself think it is—the case that nobody can escape from God. So we are forced back to thinking about the concept or picture of God. How do we think of him, how do we think he acts, what do we think that he is up to in the world? This is the sort of question to which we shall soon be directing our attention.

In the last chapter we spoke of the Christian stance and mentioned love and purpose as central in it. The Christian, we said, is one who in fellowship with others takes the attitude, adopts the perspective, in which such love and purpose are taken to be present. He is on the way to becoming the man who lives in terms of love as the meaning in the mystery of human existence, the man who finds the purpose of life in such love as more fully and widely actualized and shared.

This is the place to begin when we are talking about God and trying to form a picture of him and of his activity in the world. It is the right place for two reasons. The first is that it is the way, and the only way, in which what A. N. Whitehead once called "the Galilean vision"—the event of Jesus Christ and all that he signifies —can become dominant in our thought about God. For there, in that event, we see love in action. The second reason, more to the point in our immediate context of this worldly world, is that only when we start at that point can we begin to make God's reality a vital matter in contemporary experience. Why is this?

My answer is that even, and perhaps especially, in our worldly world, with all its scientific achievement and technical skill, love remains the "greatest" thing. Naturally I do not know how the readers of this book feel about it; but I am very much struck by the way in which young people, children of our scientific and technological culture, have rediscovered the centrality of love. They are often attacked and more often unsympathetically criticized because of their reaction against conventional ideas of respectability. These attacks and this criticism seem to me mistaken. For what I find most vital and important in their reaction is explained by their having awakened to the tremendous truth which W. H. Auden once phrased in these words: "We must love one another or die."

Deep in human experience is the need and the capacity to love and to be loved. We should not allow ourselves to be blinded by the sentimentality which so often has surrounded the word love, because in and behind that sentimentality, in and behind the romanticism and the erotic imagery so often used, there is a reality which we all need to know and which we all need to share. Someone who like myself is obliged to speak frequently to audiences of most varied types can testify that when one speaks about love, in this very profound sense, one discovers that attention at once picks up and people begin to listen. Especially when the speaker dares to use simple human analogies, such as the relationship of man and wife, lover and his beloved, of genuine caring for others as shown by good and concerned men and women, he finds that a response is almost immediately forthcoming. This is not accidental; what has happened is that the speaker has touched upon something very real and very deep in human life, not least in a time when that life has become so standardized and flat in our great urban centers.

So also we find that the songs which strike a chord, secure a response, are those that have to do with love. Many years ago, when I was young, the American composer Victor Herbert wrote a lyric with music that swept people off their feet. Its message was quite simple: "It's love and love alone the world is seeking!" In our modern worldly world, this is still true. The desire to love and to be loved, the need to love and to be loved, the joy of loving and being loved: these are things or this is *the* thing that will make sense today as it did yesterday—and as it will tomorrow. A worldly world, which with all its skills is threatened by self-destruction, is also a world in which everybody knows, if he is honest with himself, that "we must love one another or die."

3

Problems of Faith Today

In every period of Christian history, those who were seeking to become Christians have had to face problems. The most obvious problems have been of a practical sort: how to reconcile the imperatives of Christian faith, the attitudes and perspectives behind the Christian stance, with the day-to-day decisions and actions which are required if one is to live in this world at all. But there are also problems of a more intellectual sort. These can be called "theological problems," but that does not mean that they are not very real for men and women who make no profession of theological competence.

In today's worldly world, we are all faced by problems of both sorts. How are we effectively to bear witness to the Christian Way among people who misunderstand or forget what Christianity is all about? How are we to regard our own personal development as men and women of the last third of the twentieth century, in a time of technological change? How are we to reconcile the love which Christian profession demands with the establishment of justice among men and nations, between races and groups? Some of these problems and others like them will be considered as we proceed. But at the moment our attention must be turned to the "theological problems," for their importance is very real and must never be underestimated.

It may be asked why problems of this sort should interest or concern those who are not professionally engaged in theological study. Sometimes people think that theology is only a matter for specialists, who are often regarded as dry-as-dust scholars out of touch with the ordinary life of ordinary people. Of course there have been theologians who were like that; perhaps there are still some. But the theologians whom I happen to know and with whom I have worked most of my life have been very different. They have been sensitive to modern ideas, aware of modern pressures, and conscious of the fact that one of their chief responsibilities is to help work out ways of thinking about Christian faith, stating it in new terms, and relating it to contemporary issues, which will be useful for all who call themselves by the Christian name.

But theology is not really only a concern for scholars and specialists. I should be prepared to argue that every man or woman who believes in God, above all every man or woman who is trying to walk in the Christian Way and seeking to become a Christian, is by that very token a theologian. That may seem an extraordinary statement. But is it not the case that anybody who thinks at all—which means all of us, since by virtue of being human we *do* think, even if not always logically or competently—naturally tries to relate his beliefs, his convictions, the knowledge which he has, to everything else? Does he not attempt, even if in a half-conscious way, to get some kind of "big picture" of how things are and how they go in the world? Obviously most of us cannot give our whole life to this matter; equally obviously most of us will not "do theology"—for that is what we are talking about—in a skilled and professional fashion. For the most part, it is done in what I have just styled "a half-conscious way." Yet it *is* done. You have only to listen to somebody say, as I heard the other day, "Now this is how I see things . . ." and then go on to give a little sketch of how he looked at his responsibility as a Christian in respect to racial integration, to recognize that this person is really talking theology—what man is, what the world is like, what God is doing and what God requires. When somebody says, "Now as a Christian this is the way it seems to me . . ." he is speaking as a theologian—doubtless an amateur theologian but a theologian nonetheless. By the various tests of proper use of source material, logical consistency in argument, concern for rational statement, etc., he may quite likely be very amateur indeed. But he is a theologian.

For this reason I do not need to apologize for discussing with the reader, who is thus himself a theologian of sorts, two or three of the problems of faith which are of special importance today. It is the duty of those who are professionally engaged in theology to take the amateurs into our confidence and to share with them some of our thoughts. Each of us can help the others. There ought to be no "secrets" peculiar to the so-called experts. Above all, I should urge, as one who has spent his whole working life in the theological field, that the professionals can learn from the amateurs, because the latter are so close to the concrete situations in which men find themselves while there is always the possibility that the professionals may see things more abstractly and with less actual relevance to the condition of men.

The problems which we shall examine briefly in this chapter are three. First, we shall ask how we can best conceive the God whom we worship. Are we to think of him in terms of power or mind or will? Are we to focus attention on his omnipotence? Or are we to conceive of him as essentially and primarily "pure infinite love"? It is already apparent that I shall argue for the last of these. But then we must ask what difference this makes in the rest of our Christian thinking. Second, we shall ask how best we can think of the special place which Jesus Christ holds for us. In what way is he different from other instances of supposed disclosure or revelation of God in human experience and in history and nature? Third, we shall ask whether we can honestly claim that in Christian faith there is a definitive, decisive, and (as some like to say) "final" manifestation of God. If there is such, then what about the other faiths or religions by which men have lived, now do live, and doubtless will continue to live for a long time?

Here are three enormous problems selected from a considerably larger number which might well have been mentioned. The three have been chosen because it seems that they are engaging the attention of a great many Christian thinkers, while they are also implicitly present in much that is being said against Christianity by outsiders or questioners. What shall be said about each of them must be brief and tentative. In the space of one chapter it is impossible to do them justice. Yet we shall attempt to give them adequate attention, given the circumstances, and what will be said will be by way of suggestion for further thinking on the reader's part. And right here it should be added that our purpose is not to *unsettle* anybody's basic Christian faith, even when some treasured ideas are called in question; what we want to do is to deepen that basic faith, in the conviction that a thoughtless faith, which refuses to look at problems, is not likely to stand up well in today's world—or in any other world at any other time, for that matter.

The first problem is how we are to think of God—after what model are we to make our picture of him. Something has already been said about this in the last chapter. Here we must speak frankly about what some of us think to have been a very great—perhaps the greatest—tragedy in the history of Christian thought. Far too many good and wise and learned men, themselves devout Christian believers, have found that in their thinking they were unable to make absolutely central the reality of love as the very definition of God. It is easy enough for us to see why they found themselves in this position. They had inherited and they greatly respected philosophical views in which the supreme reality God was interpreted in terms of "being" or "unconditioned substance." They were the heirs of the philosophical traditions which we know as Neoplatonic and Aristotelian. For the former, God was thought to be utterly absolute, unchanged, unchangeable, untouched "being itself," self-existent and with no necessary relationships. For the latter he was taken to be "unmoved mover" who set things going in a finite world but was himself entirely impassible or unaffected by what went on there. These two models for conceiving God's nature influenced the great Christian thinkers to such a degree that they felt obliged to make pure being or substance, on the one hand, and unaffected source of change, on the other, the chief ingredients in their doctrine of God—his "root-attribute," they said, was his *aseity:* his self-existent, self-contained, self-determined reality.

Not that they forgot the revelation of God in Jesus, by which God had shown himself to be love in action. They tried to bring this glorious affirmation into relationship with their philosophical ideas drawn from nonbiblical sources. Unhappily, the two did not link up very well; and the tragedy to which I have referred was that far too often it was the nonbiblical notions which got the priority. With this was coupled still another idea. Familiar with imperial worship, with the courts of kings and emperors, many Christian thinkers took it for granted that the divine ruler of all things, God himself, was likewise to be honored and served by such servile subjection as they offered to very earthly monarchs. Omnipotence or sheer power was attributed to the One worshiped and in the presence of such power the human subject was forced to cringe in fear. This attitude was equally difficult to reconcile with the conception of God as the loving if stern Father of his children, in service of whom they found genuine freedom. There was still another element in the situation. Taught like all Christians, indeed all Jews as well, that utter righteousness characterizes the supreme God, many thinkers were unable to distinguish between that righteousness and a kind of "ruthless" moralism (to use Whitehead's adjective) whose imposition of moral requirements was arbitrary and inexplicable. Here was One who established for men commandments which were enforced by the exercise of his all-powerful will. And this too cannot easily be fitted in with the conviction that God is the understanding and loving Father whose chief interest, so far as men are concerned, is to help them become true men, in accordance with their true nature, and find joy in that becoming.

None of these ideas makes much sense, taken in the way that has been conventional, for those who see God "in the face of Jesus Christ." God, *seen there,* is not self-contained being or absolute substance; he is loving Father who ceaselessly relates himself to the world. He is not sheer omnipotence; he is the supreme Love that does not coerce but persuades, does not force but lures, does not "shove around" but attracts. He is not an imperial Caesar who demands submissive and cringing adoration; he is the great Lover who wins a response of reverence and awe precisely because he is so wonderfully good and so unfailingly concerned. Finally, he is not a moral dictator, imposing arbitrary laws which are to be obeyed at the risk of eternal damnation for disobedience; he is the "Love that will not let me go," whose whole interest is in helping his children realize fully the potentialities for good which he has implanted in them.

The only way in which the ideas just mentioned could be brought into relationship with God, it seems, was by making those ideas normative and by considering God's love as an adjective which somewhat modified the nouns "being," "unmoved mover," "omnipotent will," and "moral dictator." It is my conviction, shared increasingly by theologians of all persuasions and denominations, that things ought to have been put the other way round. That is, the great *noun* is God's love, God as Love; he is to be styled "being," "mover," "will," "moral lawgiver," only *adverbially* or *adjectivally*. Some illustrations will show our meaning. To call God omnipotent is then to say that Love such as his can never be defeated; to call him mover or creator is to say that it is Love "which makes the world go round"; to speak of him as the giver of the moral law is to say that love always expresses itself in terms of just and righteous dealings. When we affirm God's omnipresence, we are saying that the divine Love is active everywhere in the creation; when we speak of his omniscience, we say that Love is infinitely wise, penetrating into the secret hearts of men. And when we declare God's infinitude, we are insisting on the inexhaustibility of the divine Love in any and every circumstance, without the finite limits we know so well in our human loving.

Today, as we have noted, an increasing number of Christian thinkers have seen this point. They are determined that this centrality of love shall not only be dominant in their hearts but shall also be dominant in their minds as they think about the God whom they worship. A consequence of this movement has been a radical reconception of many Christian doctrines which spring from the concept of God. Everybody has heard of "radical theology"; it has been condemned and it has been praised, but its presence among us is obvious today. Those who are "radicals" are not always wise and understanding; but the one thing that is significant about them is that they are deeply concerned to stress God as "pure unbounded Love," as Wesley puts it in a familiar hymn. The solution of the first of our contemporary problems of faith has been the affirmation of God's love as first, foremost, crucial.

It is true that this solution raises still other problems, chiefly in respect to the presence of evil in the world and in human experience. We must say something about this at a later point. Here we need only remark that if the assertion of God's love aggravates for us the problem of evil, we may have one consolation. The *real* difficulty facing Christian faith is now seen, rather than a host of difficulties raised by omnipotence, sheer unrelated being, ruthless moralism—these were artificial problems, however genuine they may have seemed.

The second big issue today, we have said, has to do with the special place of Jesus Christ. There can be no question about the centrality of Christ in Christian faith. It is through his disclosure of love that the Christian attitude and perspective gets its point. To become a Christian is to "grow up into Christ." Thus one could say that Christianity *is* Jesus Christ—in him, the disciple dares claim, "God has visited and redeemed his people," because in him "the Word was made flesh and dwelt among us." Or in still another New Testament phrase, he "is the image of the invisible God." This conviction, however stated, is the clue to the meaning of Christianity. Perhaps it is expressed best of all in the first letter of John: "Herein is love, not that we loved God but that he loved us, and gave his Son." For in Jesus, God is seen as Love, cosmic Love, present with us in a genuine and complete human life.

But if this is the case, does it necessarily follow that Jesus Christ is unrelated to everything else that men have learned about God? Is he so much the great exception that other disclosures to his children, in which something of God's character and purpose have been known, are entirely pointless? Many Christians have tended to think in this way. They have said that nothing can be compared with him, nor he with anything else. He is unique in the sense of being literally the only one of the kind. Or, he is taken to be "the supreme anomaly."

The problem has lately been engaging the attention of many Christian thinkers. One factor that has impressed them has been the New Testament insistence on the full and complete humanity of Jesus. In word this has always been accepted; now it has been brought home to us in an inescapable fashion. Insofar as his manhood is concerned, Jesus is *not* separated or separable from his human brethren. But the thinkers about whom I have just spoken wish to go farther. They believe that in the activity of God which moves through that human life in Palestine there is a disclosure of what God is *always* like and what God is *always* up to in his world. What has taken place in Jesus is not to be seen as "the supreme anomaly," as if it happened but once, in that special time and place, and only there. On the contrary, Jesus is "the classical instance." In many different ways, modern thinkers have come to this view, not because it is theoretically interesting or sound, but because it is necessary if we are to interpret Jesus as genuinely the clue to God, to man, and to the relationship which properly should exist between them.

One way of putting it would be to speak of Jesus as the focus of all God-man relationship, the point where we see the truth as it really is. Thus Jesus is important and crucial because he discloses something about ourselves and about God in his dealings with us all. In disclosing this tremendous truth, he quickens men's apprehension of its significance, making it "come alive in us," awakening the response to it. By God's intention every one of his children is to become "a man in Christ," one in whom Love is at work to win the response of love.

Thus instead of talking about sharp contrasts and unbridgeable chasms between Jesus and whatever else (in persons or events) may have brought people closer to God, theologians like this wish to speak of the way in which Jesus confirms, crowns, concentrates, and where necessary corrects, everything else we know or think we know about God and his ways in the world. I believe that this is the right approach. It is different from the one that has been traditional and conventional; but it is more in accordance with the spirit of Christ himself and his welcome to all that was good and right and true wherever and however known or expressed.

Just as with our first problem, radical reconception is required once this newer attitude is adopted. For example, the way in which we talk about God's presence and action in Jesus; the way in which we think about how God redeems men through Jesus; the way in which we shall understand what an older theology styled the "benefits" of Christ (the results of his coming to us)—all these will have to be modified. Already, among the theologians to whom I have referred, this reconception and modification are going on. At the same time, the abiding *fact* of Christ, his utter centrality, and his inescapable attraction and appeal, remain entirely unchanged. The depth of Christian experience, the need for our becoming Christian men and women, the stance which gives us our grounding, are not altered. The change or alteration is in our phrasing of these things and in our way of coming to grips with their meaning.

Our third problem, it will be remembered, had to do with the Christian faith and other faiths or religions in the world. This is a pressing problem today, since in our worldly world, with its planetary sweep, we human beings are more and more living together, getting to know one another, and discovering our common humanity. There was a day when the faiths or religions of faraway people did not count for much here at home. We had heard about Hinduism, Buddhism, Islam, for instance, but we rarely if ever encountered somebody who was a convinced Hindu or Buddhist or Muslim. Now things are different. World travel, the presence of European armies or specialists in Eastern lands, the coming of Easterners to the West to study or work, in so many ways there is intercommunication and hence some awareness of other men in other lands, their cultures, their ways of life, and their religious beliefs.

In the early days of Christianity, when the new faith found itself a small minority in the great Greco-Roman world of the Roman Empire, a series of Christian thinkers, called "the Apologists," and their successors, took a surprisingly generous attitude toward much in the philosophical and religious beliefs of the time. They had no doubt about the decisive importance of their own Christian faith, but they did not deny all value to the Jewish and non-Christian ideas entertained by the great majority of their fellows. Only one or two, of whom Tertullian in North Africa is the outstanding example, were bitterly opposed to everything non-Christian. But men like Justin Martyr, Clement and Origen of Alexandria, Irenaeus of Lyons, to mention but a few, were prepared to say that something of God's grace and mercy had been disclosed to all men and especially had been revealed to the great thinkers and religious heroes outside the church. Knowing very well that Judaism had been the precursor of the specifically Christian faith, they were bound to see that God had been at work in the long history of the Jewish people. Knowing also that much in Greek and Roman thought was of use to them in understanding their own beliefs, they could not doubt that God had been at work there too. They found much to criticize in superstition, immorality, unworthy ideas of God's action and character, and occasional brutality; but they could not bring themselves to think that God had "left himself without witness" there.

Unfortunately the rediscovery of the gospel of God's free grace, at the time of the sixteenth-century Reformation, was accompanied by a hardening in attitude toward the non-Christian philosophies and faiths. There was a reason for this, of course. What was most needed just then was a vigorous reassertion of the gospel in its stark simplicity; anything that was irrelevant to *that* was rejected—and also, as we might say, under the circumstances in Europe in the sixteenth century, there was little occasion to bother about faraway religions, while philosophical ideas seemed to have been altogether too influential in the church before the reform. This negative attitude persisted for several hundred years. But now a more generous spirit has emerged and the great majority of Christian thinkers are prepared to set the Christian gospel in the context of God's whole and universal movement toward men. They do not spend their time denouncing or rejecting; they are more interested in showing how what men have yearned for, sought after, and here and there glimpsed, is fulfilled and completed in Jesus Christ.

This is why the older type of missionary, who went to some "heathen" land where people (as it was said) "fall down to wood and stone" and proclaimed Christ as the negation, denial, and destruction of everything the natives had hitherto believed, is no longer much seen. The Christian mission is now taken to be the glad sharing of life in Christ. Those who are themselves becoming Christian wish to bring others to walk in that Way. They make no claims for their own ideas; their only claim is that Jesus Christ is "the Way, the Truth, and the Life" and they invite men to accept him as such. Their mission often expresses itself in selfless service to others; only in that way can the disclosure of God as love, in Christ, be made an effective reality. Even more radically, however, many today have come to see that "the world is the missionary field"—we no longer are arrogant enough to think of the United States and Britain, for example, as "Christian countries," while India and Japan are "pagan countries." Nobody in his right mind would dare to say that his own country was a particularly "Christian" one. All of us, brethren one of another in one world, are in need both of the gospel of God's free grace and love and also of the imperative to conform our lives and actions to the implications of that gospel.

Centuries ago Ambrose said, "Every truth, wherever spoken, is spoken by the Holy Spirit." That is the attitude taken today. So also contemporary Christian leaders would agree with the ancient theologians of the church in believing that God not only has "spoken to the fathers [of Israel] in times past by the prophets" but has also disclosed himself, however dimly and partially men have responded, in every place and at every time where his children have turned to him —and often has used surprising ways of doing this.

The answer to the third problem, we may suggest, is found just there. The one Word of God—the divine self-expression to his creation—is all of a piece. That Word was given distinctive and decisive focus in Jesus Christ, but this cannot deny the fact that wherever men learn truth, create beauty, manifest goodness, seek righteousness, live honestly and bravely and decently with family and friends, and know what it means to love others and accept the love of others for themselves, that same Word has been and still is at work. Once again, however, the acceptance of this answer to the problem will entail radical reconception of much that has been conventional in Christian thought and activity. And once again, too, that is exactly what is now going on in untold numbers of places and among many Christian thinkers and practical leaders.

It ought to be apparent that in each of these problems, the new solution is related to the solutions suggested for the others. If God *is* centrally and essentially Love—and here, by the way, no single Christian in the past has been more emphatic and more convinced than the great John Wesley, whose *theological* significance has often been forgotten, even by his own followers—then it is impossible to think that he has been narrow-minded, over-selective, self-contained, or unrelated. It is impossible to think of him as limiting himself to one strand of history or to one series of human responses. "The God and Father of our Lord Jesus Christ" is nothing but "pure unbounded love"; that is "his nature and his name" and that is also the quality of his activity in the creation, in history, and in human experience. The cosmic Lover loves with passion, concern, and self-giving; he yearns for a response to his love; he rejoices when that response is made and he is in anguish when it is not made—anguish not for himself so much as because he knows that by refusing the response his children only hurt themselves.

Some may wish to say that all this is a "watering-down" of the church's historical position. How wrong can men be! Far from being a "watering-down," what has been proposed by contemporary Christian thinkers and their friends and followers is a deeper and more perceptive penetration into the very heart of the gospel. If changes are demanded, that is all to the good. For the changes will be toward a better grasp of what the church's historical faith asserts as the truth. Perhaps we may dare to say that in our own day we are witnessing another movement of the Spirit of God who is "taking of the things of Christ and declaring them unto us." This should not be an occasion for pride but a call for gratitude and thanksgiving that Christian men and women everywhere are taking with the utmost seriousness what the event of Jesus Christ manifested in concrete human act: that at the heart of things the meaning is Love and that men are given the privilege of serving as personalized instruments or channels for that Love.

One of my old teachers was in the habit of saying, "The best defense of Christianity is a reasonable and faithful presentation of it." I believe that he was correct in this judgment. What is going on in theological circles today is important precisely because it enables us to give a rational or reasonable, as well as a faithful, presentation of "the old old story of Jesus and his love"—which means *God's* love in Jesus. People today will not accept belief in God as remote, uninterested, indifferent, interfering—nor will they accept God as if he were nothing more than a concept required by the human mind if the world is to be explained. They will not accept God if he is presented as a dictator who treats men as servile subjects, demanding from them cringing submission. They have no use for God if he is regarded as morally ruthless, with no concern for the weakness and also the dignity of human life. But there is no reason why they *should* accept such a portrayal of God. *That* God is only an idol, a projection of the human mind at its worst. Indeed, he is not *God* at all. He has never existed, save in the thought of those who have wrongly taken him to be such.

The *real* God, the only God there is, the cosmic Lover who shares with his creation in its suffering and joy and who is declared for what he always is and always does in the Man Jesus, is the ground for our sense of life's significance. He is inescapable, whatever he may be called. He is supremely worshipful because he is pure and infinite Love.

4

A New Perspective:
Process and Love

We have already used the word perspective in connection with the abiding Christian stance: we spoke of attitude and perspective. The two words were intended to be nearly synonymous, when used in that context. But now we are going to use the word perspective in a different sense. What we shall be concerned with is a new and different *slant* on the one abiding Christian position, a slant which is related very intimately to the way in which we must see ourselves as those who are called to become Christians. The two aspects in that new perspective, to which we shall be giving our attention in this chapter, are indicated by the words that follow in the heading: "process and love."

Everybody is familiar enough with the notion of evolution. The word signifies change or development, in which through a long period of time things come to be what they are. It is a word which reminds us that we do not live in a world where everything is completed or finished but in a world where things "are coming to be." Originally the word evolution was used to denote biological change and the name of Charles Darwin, the great English scientist of the nineteenth century, is the symbol for this conception. Darwin showed how living creatures of all species emerge from antecedent types through a process which he named "natural selection." His work had an enormous impact when first it became known, especially when the evolutionary hypothesis—the view that change is a basic fact in the world of living matter—was applied to man and his development. Soon evolutionary ideas were applied more widely; it is now assumed by all knowledgeable people that the entire world is the field of evolutionary development, although the ways in which this occurs and the specific characteristics which mark it differ in respect to the particular subject under consideration. The evolution of a star is not identical with the evolution of living species of animals. Yet the world is seen as one in which change occurs; as I should prefer to phrase it, the world is a world which is "in process."

At one time this process was interpreted by many experts in a mechanical sort of fashion; it consisted of a reshuffling of the stuff of which the world is made, so that the possibility of genuinely *new* things was hard to maintain. In more recent times, however, full recognition is given to the novelty which appears in the course of the process of change. There is no mere rearrangement of particles of matter; there is what scientists call epigenesis, the emergence of new things with new qualities and characteristics. But this is not the place to present a detailed account of the way in which evolution or process is now understood; perhaps we may take it for granted that readers will be familiar enough with the more general picture. Our concern is to suggest how important aspects of this widely accepted notion of process make their impact upon specifically religious and Christian faith.

The first thing that must be said is that we now see that creation is not a matter of the past only. Creation is not something which was once done and is now finished. On the contrary it is a continuing activity; as we have said, things are "coming to be. . . ." This is not always apparent to the naked eye. In the subatomic field and in areas where we observe what seem to be permanent entities like rocks and hills, the presence of change is not obvious. Yet physicists tell us that formation and re-formation is always going on. The realm of the subatomic is a whirling activity of infinitesimally small entities, not something static and inert. As we mount the scale, from level to level, there is an increasing complexity in the process. Living matter is more complex than what we call inanimate matter; animals are still more complex than plants; the higher animals even more complex than the lower. In man himself, the complexity is maximal. Here we have a movement of "becoming" which is extraordinarily intense and marked by the highest degree of complex interrelationships. All the way, however, from what used to be called "matter in motion" but is now seen to be a dynamic field of energy, up to our own experience as men, there are vast numbers of routings or movements, in which each new entity builds upon its past and aims toward its future. All are in relationship with the whole cosmos in which they occur. Thus the process is not only dynamic and directional; it is also "organismic," as Professor Whitehead put it, or societal. Everything belongs together, goes together, works together, and affects and influences everything else.

Furthermore, everything has its initiating aim or direction; it is not only "coming to be," but is also "going somewhere." The acorn is on the way to becoming an oak tree; the human embryo is on the way to becoming an adult person. The creation is a creation which is going on continually, given aim and direction, moving forward to an end or purpose—even if this is not always or frequently known consciously to this or that occasion in the process.

We shall point out later, when we discuss the meaning of manhood, that it is much sounder to think of man making actual or bringing to realization the potentialities which are in him, than as a finished product of whom we may give a complete description in terms of his present obvious state. The materials provided by our past and by the past of our race, as well as by the universe of which we are part, must be in our picture. So also must be the aim toward which our development is directed. Nor can we forget the relationships with others and with the physical universe, as we grasp and are grasped by that which and those who surround us and make their impact upon us. Out of the materials of the past, through relationships in the present, and toward fulfillment of potentiality in the future: that is what a man's identity consists of. That is what each of us is. We are on the way to becoming men, as has already been said more than once in this book; we are not completed and finished specimens of manhood, ready for dissection on a laboratory table or for simple description in some textbook.

That which is true of us is true of everything else in the world. But now we must face the question: How is this change, this process, brought about? How does it come to happen? The answer here is to be found in a creative principle which provides, out of the range of possibility, the particular aim which each new entity or event is to make actual through its own free decisions. There is a continuing lure in the cosmos, eliciting from each occasion its response and inviting it to become what its initial aim makes possible for it. And once the particular event or entity has achieved fulfillment, the fulfillment is valued and preserved for use in further advance. The name which is rightly given to the creative principle that provides initial aims, lures and invites response, and receives achieved good, is nothing other than *God*. The reason it is right to use that name is plain. Relationship with and cooperation with the creative principle provides just that sense of comradeship and refreshment, just that awareness of a rightness in the grain of the universe, which religion has always denoted when the word God is used.

But God, conceived in this way, is no remote deity who occasionally intrudes into the world to make adjustments when things go wrong. He is unfailingly related to it, ceaselessly active in it. His way of working is not coercive, so much as it is persuasive and luring; he allows full freedom to each created event to say "Yes" or "No" to his invitation to follow the right and healthy line of development.

I suppose I should apologize for these last few pages, which have been abstract. The facts to which they point and which they attempt to state are anything but abstract. They are concrete, rich, complex, and familiar to each of us. When we *talk* about these matters we must necessarily seem abstract, for words can never contain, never convey, the concrete richness of experience. But the experience is very real and concrete. We know what it is like to be living, willing, feeling, sensitive, conscious men and women. We know what it *feels like* to be on the way to becoming ourselves. And the best clue to everything else in the world is to take very seriously this awareness of ourselves as "becoming." What better clue have we got?

What is more, there is every reason to do just this. For the evolutionary way of seeing things has made it plain that man emerges out of and is part of the natural order of things. Of course he is not just another thing, not just another animal; he is distinctively *himself* as a man. In him something genuinely new has appeared; as the experts put it, man is an emergent, not a mere resultant. The ordering of complexity which is specifically human is different from other orderings elsewhere in the world; human awareness and human self-awareness are of a degree of intensity which makes man different from, say, other members of the animal kingdom. So also man's moral sense of obligation or duty and his aesthetic or appreciative capacity in respect to harmony and beauty, are a novelty, not to mention his ability to engage in rational thought.

Yet at the same time he is part of the natural order of things; in the words used by a Scots thinker many years ago, "man is organic to the universe." This is why he may rightly take his own experience as a clue to what the whole creative enterprise is like. In that experience of becoming human, with sensitivity and feeling, striving and willing, awareness and self-consciousness, we have a key which can help us to see what is going on everywhere. The key should not be taken to mean that everything is identical with what we know in ourselves. That would be silly: there is no self-consciousness or sense of purpose in an electron, for example. The point is that our own experience gives us an analogy with which to work when we look at other levels or aspects of the world. Thus *something like,* although not identical with, our human aim and our human feeling-tone is found elsewhere.

The conclusion of the discussion is simply this: we can now see how very seriously we must take the dynamic view of the world and of ourselves. We must take with equal seriousness the directional aspect of things. We must see that the cosmos is getting somewhere as its various component events are more intensively knit together and work upon each other in what is a real creative advance. And we must think of *God* in that sort of context. The only possible concept of God, once the evolutionary or processive worldview has been accepted, is one that interprets him as involved in, working through, related with a world in process. So God himself shares in movement and delights in novelty. He is no great exception to a world which is going on; God himself is moving on into the future, suffering with and finding joy in the creative advance. Perhaps not surprisingly, this is how the Bible sees God, whatever may have been said about him in some traditional theologies.

The second word in the chapter title was "love." This too is part of the new perspective. Now what *is* love? We might say briefly that love is relationship in which there is the deepest and fullest sharing or mutuality. To love is to give oneself; it is also to be ready to receive from others. Thus love is essentially community or participation, where persons come together and live "in" one another. We know this from our own experience. And there is every reason to think that deep down and all the way through the processive movement of the creation, there are analogies to this too. Growing together in increasing harmony is the way the world is working. We see that the stuff of potential creativity is being patterned and ordered into various sorts of configurations, each in terms of some model of possibility—the acorn to become the oak, the embryo to become a person, to use our earlier examples. But we see also that these configurations are interdependent and interrelated; and at our human level of experience, this is nothing other than mutuality, giving-and-receiving, sharing—in other words, *love*. The drive working through the whole cosmos is a drive toward such love, to be shared as widely and completely as possible.

Modern theologians have taken this very seriously indeed. They have brought together the notion of process and the reality of love at work in the world. They have said that the evolutionary movement is a "secular" version of growth in the capacity to love and to be loved. They have maintained that this view is philosophically valid and illuminating in our effort to understand the world and ourselves. Because they are also Christians, they have said even more. They have said that the processive movement is an increasing sharing in the love which is a reflection of the very reality of God himself. God is here in the world, engaged in furthering this goal of shared love as he labors unceasingly, by lure and invitation, to bring things to make themselves—and to make themselves in community with all else that is doing the same.

It is apparent that what has now been said ties in closely with the way in which we saw, in the last chapter, that love is being taken nowadays as the supreme interpretative principle or criterion for Christian thinking. In such thinking, the conviction of love's centrality is given in the "Galilean vision," seen in Jesus Christ. The event of Christ is the norm, the focus, the point of appeal. We know what God's love is because we have known ourselves to be loved by God in Jesus: "We love, because he first loved us." The love that was "in Christ Jesus our Lord" was human love, of course, since Jesus was truly and genuinely a man. But that human love in Jesus is known through faith to be the expression or manifestation, in our own human historical terms, of the love which abides eternally in God himself—indeed, which *is* God. Thus love is the supreme causative principle in the world.

God is not only the chief causative principle, however, explaining so far as we can understand how things come to be in this processive world. He is also what Schubert Ogden, an American theologian, has well called "the supreme affect." That is, God receives into himself and is "affected by" everything that happens in the world. He cares for the world in both senses of that verb; he looks after it and he lovingly lets it influence him. If this were not the case, he would be the unreal deity who is nonrelational, remote, aloof, indifferent, and uninterested—the sort of deity whom modern people have rightly rejected as impossible and absurd. Christian faith, leading us to give ourselves to becoming Christian men, cannot allow any such idea, since it knows the divine care, the divine presence, the divine self-giving, and the way in which God shares in his creation's pain as well as in its joy in accomplishment. God, known in the actual concrete experience of faith, is always related to his world, giving to it and receiving from it. If some conventionally accepted theological systems do not say this, they are self-condemned. This *is* the God who is known to his children—and not only among Christians, either, but wherever positive religious belief has been accepted and practiced.

The insistence on process and love leads us to a deeply enriched way of thinking about God as "the high and lofty one that inhabiteth eternity"—to God in his transcendence. All too often this has been taken to suggest that God is "above the world," as if he inhabited some special supernatural realm which has little or no commerce with this one in which we live. But as Professor Whitehead once said, "God is in the world or he is nowhere." Where else *could* he be? That does not imply that the world and God are identical, as a pantheist might think; neither does it imply that God is completely and exhaustively present in the world, as those who talk of sheer immanence say. What is meant is something else. God is indeed *in* and *with* his world, yet he is *himself* too—he is God in all the fullness and amplitude of his loving nature, not "used up" (as we might phrase it) by what he does in creation, but possessed of untold resources, unexhausted and inexhaustible, the fountain-spring of life and goodness and love. He has resources adequate for handling any and every situation; he is undefeated by whatever may happen and he can never be defeated by whatever happens in the future, precisely because he is perfect in his goodness, undeviating in his purpose, and faithful in all his works.

It is my conviction that the biblical writers were saying just this sort of thing when they applied to God the most exalted terms of praise and adoration. Their way of saying it was naturally their own, characterized by the patterns of thought familiar to them. But they did not for a moment assume that there was a deity behind and beyond the God known to them in their own experience as related to them and present with them—even when they experienced his "absence" they knew that he was still there "in the shadows." They believed that Yahweh, as they called him, was their lord, to be worshiped and served in the creation which was infallibly his and from which he would never depart. At the same time, they were so much impressed and overwhelmed by his inexhaustible reality and his stupendous resources that they were bound to exalt him in language which described him as indeed "high and lofty," as "far above all things," as utterly righteous, as one upon whom men could count and in whom they could trust. He was indeed "holy," *always himself*, and men must approach him, not in cringing subservience, but in "fear and trembling."

Yet this same one God yearned for the response of his creation, which had the capacity to give a free decision for or against him and his purposes. Thus, while he was "high and lofty," he was also "near to those of a contrite heart." He was a passionate lover of his human children; his "bowels"—his deepest desire—yearned for them to come to him in love and worship him in sincerity. When Jesus came, this insight of his Jewish ancestry was taken up and further enriched, even transformed. Not only in his teaching but in his own existence as a man, those who accepted him saw there, in one who was "meek and lowly of heart," the unveiling of the innermost nature of deity. Now righteousness, justice, holiness, and goodness were all to be read in terms of a love which went to any lengths for the sake of the ones loved. There could be no doubt that God *is* Love—not the broken, frustrated, defective love which men show, but a Love which is full and strong and pure and total: *sheer Love in action.*

The new perspective which this chapter has presented makes a very great difference to us as we strive to become Christian men and women in today's world. Let me, for once, be personal about this. I have always been a Christian and I have spent most of my life as a Christian theologian. But it was only when I came to realize that I am living in a world which is a dynamic movement of creative advance that I began to see what it *means* to be growing in Christian discipleship. My slight growth was part of an enormous process in which God was at work, not just in my own life but everywhere and always. He was inviting and luring me and everything else to become that which he purposed us to be, instruments for his loving concern. But because he was indeed "pure unbounded love," he would not coerce or force me in any way. He invited and solicited my response, but he left me free to make it for myself. I began to grasp the truth that God was no remote deity who was unconcerned about the world and who could not be affected by what went on there. Yet he was no ruthlessly exacting moral tyrant, either, exerting pressure on me and his world to do his righteous will. He had set things in such a fashion that to do his will *was* to become myself; to fulfill my own potentialities, with free choices made in the light of the best I knew, was nothing other than to be God's personalized instrument of love in the world. Furthermore, I was with others in this enterprise; we were all knit together in a comradeship where each was to help all and where all helped each one.

The sense of freedom and release which this new perspective gave me was quite literally marvelous. I found myself not more a Christian than before, but more aware of what was involved in becoming the Christian I so much desired to be. I came to understand why the Christian gospel is sheer liberty—not license, mind you, for it controls life in the light of the best and truest and finest possibilities, but liberty which is the freedom for realizing one's real selfhood. Because I have known all this in my own experience, I am anxious to share it with others. That, indeed, is why I have written just *this* book and not a book of another kind.

In the chapters which follow we shall start from this point. That is, we shall assume a processive world in which there is nothing that is fixed or static. We shall take for granted a world in which change, development, alteration, are continually going on. This does not mean that we shall also think that there are no abiding realities or truths, but it means that such abiding things have their identity not in some dead structure which permits of no alteration but in a direction taken, a routing known, and a line followed. Identity can be found in change, when there is such a consistent direction or routing or line; it is a fallacy to think that only the inert or utterly changeless is abiding in significance, purpose, and meaning. Such an idea is one of the sad legacies of a philosophical view which simply assumed, without inquiry, that the static is better than the changing, the absolute better than the relative, and being better than becoming. We happen to think otherwise—and so do most of our contemporaries, although they could not argue their case in a theoretical fashion.

Furthermore, in what follows we shall assume that ours is indeed a worldly world, in which human responsibility is taken for granted and in which human knowledge is not thought to be a blasphemous violation of divine prerogatives but a gift for men to use. We shall assume that it is man's duty to make the best of and do the best with the situation in which he finds himself as a limited, finite, mortal creature who in a serious sense has "come of age." Most important of all, we shall take as our chief article of faith the conviction that God is Love and hence that love is the meaning of the mystery of human existence and of the world where that existence is lived out. This will mean that in every question we look into and in every aspect of experience which we try to interpret, we shall look for the purpose of love, not always obviously present and certainly not always plainly visible, yet running through all things. Only on the basis of this series of assumptions can we claim to be seeing the world and ourselves in a genuinely Christian way, alert to the times in which we live but undeviating in our allegiance to the "love of God which was in Christ Jesus our Lord."

The next chapter will consider what may be said about human nature, what it means to be a man. This will lead us to look at the human response to how things are and how they go in the world, with the responsibility laid upon us to work together with the movement of love which is God in his action in creation. Succeeding chapters will look at the way toward human maturity, the authentic human living proper to those who are becoming Christians. This will lead naturally to a consideration of the significance of human sexuality, since whatever else may be true about man his sexual desire and drive is most certainly a dominant factor in his existence. In the final chapters we shall turn our attention to the agelong practice of prayer and worship in an effort to see what this may mean in the light of our new perspective; and then speak of "the end," the question of human destiny and how best we can make sense of what the historic tradition tells us about it. A closing chapter will try to sum up what we have been urging throughout the book and to give some very simple and practical hints as to ways in which this may "come alive" in our daily living.

5

Becoming Truly Human

It may seem a little silly to put it in just this fashion, but the answer to the question "What is the purpose of human existence?" is simply this: "The purpose of human existence is to become human." That is *God's* purpose for man, as Paul Lehmann has said in his book *Ethics in a Christian Context:* "to make and to keep man human." Hence that is also man's own purpose.

The answer seems tautological, of course—it simply repeats the question as it has been phrased. But we shall see that this is not really the case. In this chapter we intend to unpack that simple answer, in an attempt to show how significant and far-reaching it is. *To become a man:* that vocation is enough to engage all our time and take all our effort, our specific jobs and responsibilities all playing their part to that end. So also our human relationships, with persons loved, with family, with friends, associates, and people more remote from us, are factors in this growth into true manhood. Indeed everything that happens to us, as well as everything we do, has its contribution to make here.

First of all, however, we must recognize that in a perhaps surprising way man has always been a problem to himself. A familiar story tells of the German philosopher Schopenhauer who was sitting one day on a bench in the park of some city. Since he was not well-dressed and was lost in thought, a policeman took him to be a shifty vagabond. Going over to him, the policeman asked, "Who are you? what are you doing here?" To which the philosopher replied, "I would to God I knew . . ."

Who we are, what we are doing here, these are the two big questions every man is obliged to face and answer. Of course the questions do not always, or often, come to us plainly, nor do we ask them painfully. We feel only a certain concern, maybe a slight disquiet. When things are going well with us, we do not bother much. But there are the moments when we *do* bother. Late at night when we are unable to get to sleep we may wonder about it all. When life is "too much" for us, as we say, or when we have had a great disappointment or feel rejected by a friend or a loved person on whom we had thought we could count, we ask ourselves what life means and who we really are. We demand some sort of answer. To fail to find one is to have a sense of emptiness and to lack a motive for living. The one thing that differentiates men from every other species known to us, is the capacity to ask questions like this, that have to do with *meaning*. Dogs and cats, horses and cows, do not do this, so far as we can gather. *We* do. We may not put it in such a violent manner as Schopenhauer; nonetheless, "We would to God we knew" who we are and why we are here.

Well, who am I? The only way to arrive at an answer is by looking at ourselves in the setting which is ours as men, and as the children of God. If I am a child of God, his son, then I can only understand myself as one of a great family of sons who have been created to live in the kind of world which is ours for the purpose of fulfilling God's plan. More of this will become clear as we proceed. At the moment, the point to be made is that the question of my identity as a man is really a question about the *significance* of my life in the grand purpose of the world as a whole. Living in such a processive world, called upon to accept responsibility, what is my significance? The same sort of approach is required when we ask what we are here for. As a matter of fact, the two questions are really different ways of asking the same one question, which is the question about the significance of human life—how it fits in with, is given sense by, and finds its true value in the ongoing movement of this world of ours, its creative advance in and under the power of God's love.

As we begin our discussion of man, there are two or three points that ought to be made clear. The first has to do with what a human being is "made up of," as we might phrase it. Certainly I am not a pure spirit or pure mind. Of course I can think. I am a reasoning being, to a greater or less degree. But to say that I *am* "a mind" would be to assume that I live only in the realm of intellect. In the same way, to talk of myself as "a spirit" would indicate that I lived in some realm of spiritual reality and only happened, for the time being, to be "attached" to a body. But I am not *just* a body and nothing more. I live in a physical world and I have a physical body. I express myself through that body and I receive all I know from contacts which my body makes or ways in which my body functions. In one sense I am a complicated physical organism. Yet I am more than that, since I can know myself, think about myself, "get out of myself" (as we say) and look at myself: "I" know "me," think about "me," look at "me." This is a strange fact about myself but it is inescapable. What I seem to be is a very complex society of factors mental and physical; somehow these are in a unity of such a sort that the mental affects and is affected by the physical and vice versa. I am a thinking, yearning, willing, desiring organism, knowing myself to be such, and there is within me a striving for something "more" than I already am or possess.

In the second place, I am part of the human race. This is no mere accident of my existence, which I could do without. On the contrary it is an integral and essential part of that existence. I belong with my fellowmen in a way which is much more significant than simple physical dependence upon them for food and shelter and the other necessities of life. Try as hard as I may, I can never succeed in being an insulated individual, separated from my brethren. To want to be like that is to try to avoid the facts of the situation. I may fool myself about the matter, pretending that I have thus separated myself; but I can never really do it. Even when I am not in the actual presence of other men I am still part of the race of men. I belong to that human solidarity. The Old Testament has a fine text which expresses this truth about men: it says that we are "knit together in a bundle of life."

This relationship with my fellows has its roots deep in the past and its ramifications everywhere in the present. I am tied in with that part of mankind to which I immediately belong. But I am also part of the whole contemporary human condition which has its own roots in the past. When I forget this, as I often do, the influence of others is still there to be reckoned with, even if it is present in subtle ways that are not always easily observable. To be a person *is* to be a social animal, so to say; personality and "sociality" belong together. Part of the dignity of man is that his belonging to his race is not simply a gross fact, but may be consciously apprehended and acted upon. The development of personality is the ground for this awareness; and conversely, as the psychologists now tell us, my own self-consciousness has come into existence through the presence of others—the baby learns to be a self because he is aware of *other* selves with whom he must have to do.

If physical existence in a body and corporate existence in a common humanity are integral to manhood, so is another environmental pressure which nobody can escape. This is the movement in and upon us of whatever-it-is that is going on in the world at large; in the final analysis, it is the movement in and upon us of the ultimate reality or creative principle in the process of change and development. For Christians this ever-present fact is seen to be nothing other than God himself as he works in the world. God is the dynamic power in the world—and unexhausted by the world, too, as we have seen when we were speaking of transcendence—which is ceaselessly laboring to bring everything to its fullest possible actualization of potentiality. The world is the place where this occurs. And since the ultimate end or purpose in view is love shared as widely as possible, the pressure upon man is to participate in this love in action. That is what the whole enterprise is about; that is the direction in which we see the world moving. Hence whatever is said about myself must be said in the light of that all-encompassing thrust in the cosmos, in the world of nature, in history, and in human experience. Dominant in it, as sovereign ruler whose action is by persuasion and lure rather than by coercion and sheer power, is God himself. He is with his creation as "the fellow-sufferer who understands," as Whitehead put it on one occasion; he is the supremely excellent and altogether wonderful summation of all that is good. He *is* Love, working in love and for love to secure a response of love from his creation and especially from the conscious and appreciative part of it, the race of men.

In this context, then, I can begin to answer the question "Who am I?"

I am a self-conscious, feeling, desiring, willing, and thinking identity, a routing of experiences and occurrences, in the process of being created as a personal instrument for the dynamic love of God. In becoming such a personal instrument, I am on the way to becoming a lover, finding my fulfillment and satisfaction in the sharing and mutuality which is love. I am becoming what I am called to become:

a man. Furthermore, since I have come to know the gospel of Jesus Christ, in whom God as Love is focally expressed in the human situation, I am becoming—if I will choose to have it so—"a man in Christ," as Paul put it. That is to say, a man in whom the self-same love of God, brought to bear on the human condition in the man Jesus, is effectively at work and may effectively be released into the affairs of the world.

Of course I am *not* Jesus Christ. His identity is his own; so is mine. But by the interpenetration of personality which is so wonderful a reality in our human experience, he can "live in me and I in him." His bringing of the divine Love can influence and affect *me*. To let it do so is what it *means* to be on the way to becoming a Christian; this *is* the Christian Way, pioneered by the Lord who also companies with those who walk in it.

I have said, "If I choose to have it so." That brings before us the very important matter of human freedom in decision. My decisions are my own; they belong to nobody else, not even to God. I am no part of God even if he is at work in my life. I cannot blame him for what I myself decide, nor does he claim credit for the decisions which he has left me free to make on my own responsibility. If I refuse the positive response to God's lure, inviting me to realize my capacity to grow in love, then I am in the position which traditional theology calls "sin." I am making myself an enemy of God. That would be bad enough if it affected me only. But because of the communal or social nature of human personality, my wrong decisions also influence others. For centuries, indeed for his whole history of decision, man has made such wrong decisions. The cumulative result is a situation in which the making of right decisions, those *for* rather than *against* love in action, becomes more difficult for everybody. Just as the "decisions" made in other levels of creation, physical and inorganic and organic, decisions analogous to but of course not identical with human self-conscious choice, can and do establish backwaters, deviations, drags, and distortions making the creative advance more difficult but never completely impossible; so, at the human level, the story of man is in one sense a story of wrong decisions which prevent God's perfect will of love being done completely. The story, however, is also of God's loving care for and his providing ways in the creation and in human life, whereby evil and sin are used as means to a greater good. For a Christian, the tragedy of Good Friday, overcome in the victory of Easter Day, is the paradigm or illuminating model for this profound truth.

We have now begun to understand the significance of human life —what it means to be on the way to becoming truly human. It is exactly what the New Testament calls growing up "into the measure of the stature of the fullness of Christ, into a perfect man." In a world such as ours, where nothing continues "fixed" and where all is movement and dynamic change, the task which is ours is what constitutes us as men. We do not have an identity over and above, or different from, the movement or routing of experience and happening of which we are composed. The sophisticated way of saying this is to assert that a thing *is* what it is seen *to do* or finds itself *doing*. A philosopher would put the same truth if he wrote that "ontology" is determined by "function." If we are to become consciously and intentionally the personalized channels of the cosmic thrust of love, that is not only our task; it is also our purposed identity. And if it be the case that full manhood, after the model of Jesus Christ, is creaturely love in action, then the meaning or significance of our manhood is clear enough. In the span of years which is our mortal existence, we are given the opportunity to let this happen. We are to strive toward it, but we know that our striving is but a responsive movement to a love which has grasped us before ever we sought it. In one of the apocryphal books of the Bible, God is called "lover of souls"; what a splendid phrase that is! As such, he loves us into existence and then lures us to share with him in the effecting of more love in more places and at more times for more people and in more ways. That is our calling; in answering the call we find our human dignity as God's sons.

If this is true of each of us personally, it is also true of the human race as a whole. Mankind is created to become a loving community. As we shall see in a moment, this has not yet been achieved, nor is it likely to be perfectly achieved in the finite existence we know. But this is the aim or goal. The consequences of this insight into the purpose of the human race are enormous. Every human problem is illuminated. To take a crucial contemporary example, racial relations can never be put on the right basis if it is only abstract justice which is sought or given. That is important enough, to be sure. Yet underneath justice must be the foundation of common understanding; and the condition of common understanding is an attitude of generous self-giving which is love in action. The white man must give the black man the justice which he demands. But until the white man also cares for the black man, in no spirit of condescension but in an openness which is ready to receive as well as give, and until the black man has the same care for the white man, racial relations may be improved and made more decent, but they will not be *right*. What is true in this particular instance is equally true of other human relationships between groups and classes, between nations, and between people of different cultures and history. Love must be "at the roots"; justice will then be a way in which love is expressed.

We can now come to recognize that the human community is not simply an aggregation of vast numbers of individuals, neither is it a generalized and amorphous superentity destructive of the specific characteristics of those who compose it, like an ant heap. It is a genuine society or interrelationship of men and women who are knit together in the most intimate fashion. To say *that* is also to say that the human community has a purpose which is not apart from but located in the purpose of those who make it up. Its dignity, like theirs, is to serve as a preparation for the realm of love in act which the Bible calls "the kingdom of God."

Further, we are now able to see that the true worth of human society, like that of each member of it, is not because there is something "holy" about manhood as such. From one point of view, naturally, we could say that each man, like an individual dog or cat, is expendable. He is only one of a kind and there is no reason to assume that he must be treated in special esteem. *But* there is something "holy" about each man, as well as about the community of men, if and when it is seen that they are divinely indwelt, divinely employed, and able to contribute to the divine fulfillment of aim—that is, when they are lovers of the kind we have urged and are called to become more and more the instruments (fully personal and free) for the expression of the divine Love in the world's affairs.

We have talked much about man's deepest intentionality as a lover in the making, one who is becoming such an instrument for love, hence becoming a man in the true sense. But am I really on the way? Can I honestly make any such claim?

Surely the answer must be both "Yes" and "No." It is "Yes" in that this is my God-purposed meaning and destiny; this *is* my significance as a man. So we have argued and I do not wish to retract a single word that has been said. Yet there is also the "No." The reason for this is that my loving is both frustrated by conditions and circumstances over which I have little if any control *and* is also deficient, distorted, and deviant by my own free choice as a member of the human community. The traditional religious word for this human situation is "sin." We may not like the word, especially nowadays when it is so frequently misinterpreted. But the fact to which the word points is a tragic and terrible reality which no honest man can deny. Men *are* sinners. They live in a world where through long accumulation of wrongdoing, deviating from the purpose of love, and because of the continuing decisions which are for far less than the truest good, they violate the relationship of open fellowship between their God and themselves. Not only this, but they violate the relationship which is intended for them with their fellowmen. In one way worst of all, they violate *themselves;* for surely a most frightful violation of selfhood is seen when a man chooses the narrow, falsely selfish and self-centered way, preferring this to the direction which is inclusive, open, shareable, thoroughly in accord with the purpose of love, divine and human.

For this state, each of us is responsible. Of course there are aspects or elements in the situation which are not our own fault. If I live in Boston I am different from what I would be if I lived in Tibet; my possibilities of choice are different too. There are factors such as climate, natural resources, family inheritance, social environment, and the like, over which I personally have no control and which play their part in frustrating me. What is significant here is what *I do* in the midst of these frustrations. How do I handle them? What is my attitude toward them? But in the areas where my own choice is effectual, I have a responsibility which is inescapable. If I am by divine intention and by the purposed direction of my human becoming a lover in the making, I am both a frustrated lover and a sinful (or defective and self-willed) lover.

The requirement to give this partial "No" is not pleasant. Nor is the reality which demands that we give that answer pleasant either. Let no one minimize the horror of human sin. On the other hand, it serves no good purpose when we stress sin so much that the creaturely goodness in man, along with his potentiality for growing in love and hence becoming truly human, is forgotten or neglected. In some traditional theologies this latter has been done, to such a degree that they have seemed to turn the gospel of God's free grace into the story of man's wickedness—and that is to turn the whole Christian enterprise upside down. The gospel, it has been said, is not about "the old Adam in whom we die" but about "the new Adam in whom we are made alive." The point here is that the Christian proclamation is concerned with what human life may become "in Christ," rather than with the distortions, deviations, and frustrations which we know so well and which can discourage us and put us in utter despair. We are delivered from such despair and discouragement about ourselves, our neighbors, and the world, when we respond to the Love which in Christ comes to meet us, dwell with us and within us, and make us whole and new. This is indeed *gospel,* that is to say "good news."

When one speaks of "deviations," in this matter of sin, it is necessary to be a little careful. Alas, the word has come to mean for a great many people the sort of behavior pattern that is not agreeable to respectable citizens. Thus the hippie is thought to be a deviant from the norm of conventional society. The homosexual man or woman is said to be guilty of deviation from the general acceptance of heterosexuality as proper for every human being. It is not of such "deviance" that we are speaking here—and I myself could not agree that the hippie, on the one hand, or the homosexual, on the other, is rightly called by any such name. Such persons are indeed different from the vast majority; but there is no reason to assume that they are in deviation more than are the rest of us, in the most profound sense of that word deviation. What is that sense? Surely, as our argument ought to have made plain, it is found in the choice to live narrowly, to avoid loving where love is most needed, to seek one's own preference while forgetting others—in short, to fail in expressing the goodness or love which is possible for us. *That* is deviation of the most terrible sort; *that* is distortion of human nature. That is *sin.* We all know people who are like that; what is more, we know that we ourselves are like that too. If I look at my own life I have no doubt at all that I have failed most dreadfully as a lover in the making—and it has been my own fault for which I must assume full responsibility.

Sin, therefore, is not breaking an imposed moral code which has been handed down from on high. It is exactly what we have called it above: violation of relationships in love. This makes it all the more terrible and all the more serious too. If sin were simply a matter of disobeying a legal requirement, we might easily find excuses. That is what a good deal of legal practice is concerned to do. But when sin is the violation of loving relationships, we cannot take refuge in easy excuses for our self-chosen refusal to love in the fullest sense possible to us in any given circumstance. We know perfectly well that we could have loved more and better than we did, however restricted may have been the area of our loving and however limited the channels through which that loving might have been manifested. No honest man or woman, looking seriously at his own life, will disclaim this measure of responsibility. To do so would be to admit that he is not on the way to manhood but is so immersed in the negativities of his present existence that he has lost the vision of his future goal.

Some may think that this talk of love is only sentimentality. But I hope that I have made it apparent to the reader that the love with which Christians have to do is a strong and virile love, as well as a passionate and concerned love. It is not a matter of soft emotion or easy toleration of whatever happens to seem (for the moment) nice and comfortable. There is self-giving here, which entails sacrifice. There is receiving, which shatters our pride. There is mutuality, which demands our sharing with others at cost to ourselves. There is the awful anguish known when love is rejected or denied. The picture which we should have in our minds is Calvary, where Jesus "having loved his own which were in the world, loved them unto the end." And the writer of John's Gospel intends to tell us, by those words, that he loved to the point of death. Such love is not sentimental or sloppy or soft; it is the strongest thing in the world.

Failure in love, with the disharmony which follows, is responsible for the sense of alienation that marks so much of human life; it is also the chief element in the meaninglessness which attaches to human existence when no genuine purpose for that existence can be found. But surrender to the imperative of love is not only redemption from alienation and meaninglessness. It is also the inspiration for the concern with other people which is the presupposition for all effort to better their lot. The social implications of such love are enormous; as this is recognized by more Christians today, they are impelled to join in the struggle for justice at every level and in every place. Conventional Christians of the pietistic type are sometimes dismayed at this zeal for "social action" and think that it reduces the reality of the personal relationship of man with God, sinner with his Savior. But exactly the reverse is true, if the writer of the first letter of John knew what he was talking about. Those who love God must love their brother also—and to love one's brother is to care for him, to seek his best good, and to do all in one's power to give him that which is his human due.

We have insisted that human life is not a thing but a process. In this respect it is like everything else in creation. A man is not a fixed entity, as if he could be pinned on a board and studied like some specimen in a museum. He is living, moving, directional, a series of routings with identity rather than an object. Each of us comes into existence with possibilities that are open to us; we have an aim which we are to actualize—to become truly human. Our past is always with us and we remember it in a sense much more serious than simple, conscious recollection; it is embedded in our cells, our viscera, the whole bodily stuff of which we are made, as well as in our memory in the usual meaning of the word. Each of us is related to the world of nature, made up as we are of the same materials as are studied by the chemist and functioning in ways that the biologist, physiologist, physicist may observe. We have our emotions and yearnings, our desires and strivings, as we have also our capacity for thought and reason. We live with others of our race, inheriting from the common past and associated in the common life of the human community. We aim toward future goals, seeking to realize these as best we can however dimly or vaguely may be our awareness of them.

Out of the stuff of which he is composed, with his deeply remembered past; in the relationships which he sustains in the present, grasped by them and grasping them in their two-directional significance; with his capacity to know and understand, to appreciate and value, to desire and yearn both to give himself and to receive from others; and possessed of an aim or goal toward the realization of which he is drawn—here is the material, so to say, out of which the human loving instrument for cosmic Love is being made. And a man *lives* to the degree in which this process of becoming takes place during his mortal existence. Otherwise, he is sinking to the level of meaningless, insignificant, pointless being—and it is in his becoming, *not* in his being, despite a long tradition in Western thought, that his glory and dignity consist. Ramón Lull, the Spanish mystic of the Middle Ages once said, "He who loves not, lives not."

It is no accident that the songs which appeal most to the human heart are songs that speak about love and about loving. Nor is it only modern popular lyrics which do this. The old ones are equally eloquent of the human desire for and need of love. "All the world loves a lover," the saying goes. It is right in saying it, since the world of men is composed of lovers, lovers in the making, lovers who are frustrated in their loving, lovers who by their own choice and because of the choices of other men are distorted in their loving, but lovers, nonetheless. The love about which the songs tell us is not always joyous, in a superficial sense, nor is it only a matter of pleasure. It is a love which is marked by pain and suffering. For there is anguish in true love, as everyone who has loved knows full well.

In the Italian tongue there is the word *dolore* which is often associated with the experience of love. That word can mean suffering, pain, illness, distress, or anguish; it has nuances of meaning that are untranslatable. Love does include *dolore*. Its deepest note is unspeakable joy, but in and through and with the joy there is the necessity of separation, dreams of fulfillment which have failed, the pain which results from our inability ever to be entirely one with the loved person. Thus human life is no mere accumulation of pleasures. But nobody in his senses would ever have thought that it was. I say this because I am quite sure that our truest human wisdom comes to us in the moments when we suffer "the pains of love," although we may also learn wisdom in the hours when we are supremely happy.

Why the world is so constituted, *why* God himself is caught up in suffering as well as joy, *why* this is true also of ourselves, we cannot say. Here is a point where we come to the last irrationality, the inexplicable which we must accept whether we like it or not. Yet we *can* discern that a world like that, a God like that, and human experience of that order, provides a fit field for the making of lovers. The result is worth the cost. And certainly we cannot conceive a higher destiny for man than to become what he is being created for: the fully personalized channel through which love is effectively at work. Nor can we conceive a finer or nobler picture of God than the cosmic Lover who participates in his world, lives with his children in all their joy and pain, and gives himself to the limit that they may become his faithful children.

6

Response and Responsibility

In the last chapter we argued that man is being created—not *has been created*, for that would suggest that he is already a finished product—to become truly human. The purpose of man, we said, is to become a man. And we went on to urge that to say this is at the same time to say that man is to become a lover, who as a personalized instrument or channel of the divine Love, in company with his brethren, is to find his meaning in sharing good with others in as many ways and places and times as are open to his action.

Since this is man's true significance, he must find his existence in the response which he makes to every invitation and opportunity for loving, caring, having concern, and sharing good. We live in terms of such responses, while we have also our own initiating capacity to act in such a fashion that response will be evoked from others. That is just a way of saying that human life, like everything else in this processive and organic or societal world, is *in relationships*. Even for God himself, I have been bold to claim, this is true. He does not "exist" or "subsist" in isolation from his world; he is not entirely self-contained, the absolute without relationships. On the contrary he exists as God in his relationships with that which is not himself— with the world. In scripture, God is highly exalted and praised as altogether adorable; but nothing is said about him which would make us think that he can be approached or known, nor that he *is*, save in his ceaseless action in the creation. This is why we can properly call him Love and speak of him as the cosmic Lover.

As to man, relationship is so important for him that a human being who is deprived of such contacts becomes neurotic, maybe even psychotic. He begins to lose his distinctive manhood as personality-in-making and becomes a miserable, withdrawn, and lonely creature. Man only can *become*, as I have continually phrased it, when he responds to the influences which press in upon him, while in his own outgoing he expresses what he is becoming and awakens in others the responsivity which must be theirs.

When Jesus said that we are to "be perfect," as our Father in heaven is "perfect," he was not talking about some abstract perfection, existing in lily-white purity apart from others. He was urging his hearers to "imitate God," as we can put it. God *is* in his rich relationships; that is his perfection—the capacity to be open and free, to enter into contact with the world, to be affected by it, and yet to remain himself. Men are to be like him and they are enabled to come to this likeness through the persuasive pressure of God's love, moving toward them and in them through what happens to them and what is made available for them.

In the English language the two words "response" and "responsibility" are closely related in meaning, although this is not always recognized. The same is true in many other languages, in some of which indeed the connection is even plainer. Here, as so often, the way people talk and the words they use in talking may indicate something very important about them. We talk as if we had laid upon us an obligation to make a response to others. We talk as if in making that response we had the duty to make it in full integrity and with a profound awareness of what is due to others. Deep in human life is this drive to become more fully human by a genuine and loyal response made to others. That entails the sense of responsibility which we assume for others with an obligation to care for them, make the best use of the possibilities of our common "togetherness" (to use for once this popular word), and thus to promote so far as we are able the fullest development of the world of persons and things toward its intended goal. We have stressed what that goal comes to: a growing community of love, under God who is its "King," as the Bible says, but whose royal rule is the rule of love in action and not the tyrannical dictate of an oriental sultan.

It is obvious that we have returned to the point made earlier in our discussion when we quoted the now familiar words of Dietrich Bonhoeffer, that man is "come of age" and must act on that basis. As we saw, Bonhoeffer did not intend the absurd idea that the human race is entirely "grown up" and mature in every way. He was insisting that the race of men has gone beyond infancy, childhood, or adolescence; hence it must know its responsibility for human existence and for the kind of world in which that existence may properly be lived out. The child or early adolescent cannot make any such assumption. The child is too ill-informed; while the adolescent must struggle to learn, and earn, the privilege of responsibility. Those who have not "come of age" lack the experience and knowledge which full responsibility requires. It is perfectly proper for a child or an adolescent to turn to his father for advice, for help under almost any circumstance, and for refuge when things get too difficult. But there comes a time, as every father knows, when the son must take upon himself the duties of manhood; the son knows too that he must accept the obligations that this "coming of age" entails. This is our human situation in the world. God does not treat us as babies or adolescent children, any more than he treats us as slaves. He treats us as his sons and he rejoices when we act as responsible sons.

The truth here indicated might well be put in story form. Once upon a time, we may say, men were children who needed to be guided and led every moment of their lives. They were not sufficiently instructed, nor did they have sufficient strength to face the demands which life made upon them. But as the years went by, they came to learn more and more, while their strength grew too as they were hardened in body and mind. God did not wish it otherwise. He tended and cared for his children when they were young, but it was not his purpose to keep them in their perambulator forever, nor did he desire that they should continue to be so completely dependent upon him that in their late adolescence they were not permitted to make any decisions of their own. What God wanted was the slow but steady growth of his children toward true manhood, to the point where they could be trusted to act for themselves in a responsible manner.

Throughout their development God cared for them, loved them, surrounded them with insistent pressures for good, and worked persuasively for their best growth. Like a wise parent he continued to do this when finally they came to the age of relative manhood. He did not continually interfere with them, try to shove them around or push them about; he never took from them their independence, nor did he demand that they obey him without question. He always had a reason for what he did and he wanted his children to understand that reason. He was too loving and wise to attempt to coerce those whom he loved—that would have been self-defeating anyway, since a coerced response is not really a human response at all but is like the automatic reaction of a robot. It is simply impossible to *make* somebody "good" or to compel him to love you. Submission in a servile fashion is anything but response; it never includes the person in the act.

The "professional moralists" do not understand this obvious truth. They tend to assume that if somebody is coerced into "going through the motions," sufficient response has been made. But of course this is not the case, as we all know. That situation would be like forcing somebody into the similitude of the act of love—it would be rape, in which there is love on neither side. God's way of winning his children is precisely in his treating them as "come of age," respecting their freedom and influencing them by his caring concern and his insistent yet persuasive pressures toward fuller realization of their manhood. The divine patience here is inexhaustible. Unlike you and me, God never gives up when the going is difficult. On the contrary, he cares all the more and loves the more deeply. What is even more significant, God has "all the time there is" to carry out this purpose of his. Our perspective is short-range and limited; his view is long-range and is inclusive of all possibilities of good for us and for everything else in his world. He can afford to be patient, since the good which he wants to share is a good which in the long run is not only *his* but is also ours. His urgent desire to win us to that good is his glory revealed; it is also our satisfaction achieved.

In this process of our becoming truly human, the lovers we are meant to be, we have our specific human responsibility as we respond in our various ways to what goes on in the world and as we act in the world to awaken response from others. The first of our human duties is of course just our becoming what it is in us to become. We fail in this respect—we sin. But God does not let matters rest there. Despite our distortions and deviations or sin, he continues to care for us, taking us just as we are and where we are, accepting us even in our sin yet seeing in us the possibilities that are latent and that can be brought to flower. His love for his children is expressed, perhaps above all, in this readiness to accept us although we are obviously unacceptable. The German-American theologian Paul Tillich stressed this, pointing out that precisely when a man knows himself to be unacceptable, even by himself, he is still accepted by God and thus is enabled to accept himself, others, and his situation. This is what forgiveness is all about: it is prospective in reference, taking men for what they may become rather than for what at the moment they happen to be like. That also is the point of the doctrine of "justification by grace through faith," which (as Martin Luther saw) is "the article of a standing or falling Church," the one great affirmation which indicates whether or not the Christian community has really grasped the gospel of God's free love in Jesus Christ.

When God accepts us, he accepts us "in Christ"—so the New Testament declares. That is to say, he accepts us as being already "in love" or as lovers, when as a matter of observable fact we are nothing like that at all. "While we were *yet* sinners," Paul tells us, God loved us and saw us as being "in Christ." So he who comes to us in love in that same Christ acts to make us sharers in the love which *is* Christ and hence to become our true selves. That is how cosmic Love works; that is what cosmic Love intends.

Our specifically human responsibility is first of all to become true men. But it does not stop there. God's purpose and plan, which is also our goal and our responsibility, is that each man shall feel the need to care for other men. We are to be "for others," as the radical theologians are today reminding us. Martin Luther put this in saying that each man is to be "a Christ" for his neighbor; through him the loving concern of God, focused as it was in Jesus of Nazareth, is to flow out to those whom he meets, with whom he works, and for whom he can act. Thus our second area of human responsibility is in caring for, aiding and comforting, urging and influencing our fellows. This has its immediate application in those who are in close contact with us, in our families, our neighborhood, our companions in work and play. But it also has to do with those with whom our contact is more remote. Our fellow-citizens at home and people living in far distant places are included. But whether near or far, the relationship of man to man is real and the responsibility of man for men is equally pressing. There is no escape here, save by abdicating our manhood.

Each of us needs continually to ask himself what he is doing about such responsibility for others. In the several circles of contact, close or distant, do I find myself really caring? How ready am I to give what help I can? Are my contacts narrowly restricted to a very few or do I try to refuse all contacts whatsoever? Or do I seek to broaden these contacts, so that they may become more inclusive of others and in consequence more demanding upon me? Do I try to be alert to the needs of others and where possible make my contribution to the relief of those needs?—not just the physical needs, either, but the emotional and mental and spiritual needs of men. Do I let myself imaginatively enter into their lot, put myself in their place, and try to grasp how they feel and think? This sort of question can be very searching. Once we have begun to ask it, we know our inadequacy but we will find ourselves moved to a renewed sense of our responsibility.

Our attitude toward all these others is meant to be a reflection of *God's* attitude to them. As I was writing these words in Rome, I heard on the Italian radio a folk song from the United States, whose message (sung poignantly in the recording I heard) was that since "there's not enough love to go round," we must all try to show sympathy and understanding one for another. Certainly the responsibility of men, reflecting God's attitude, is to show such sympathy and understanding. But the earlier phrase in the song, while true enough so far as observation of human conduct tells us, is not true from the perspective of Christian faith. There *is* "enough love to go round," precisely because God *is* love and his love is everywhere, at every time, and for all men. Yet the responsibility which is ours as men, in relation with our fellows, is to demonstrate by what we say and do that love, love like that, does indeed "go round"; it is the privilege of men, above all of men who are becoming Christian, to be the channels of that love.

In thus assuming responsibility for others we must accept them as they are and where they are, confident of the God-implanted potentialities which are theirs and setting ourselves to do all in our power to assist in the realizing of these potentialities. The cosmic Love is then really at work in us, as we respond responsibly to others in their need. We are letting ourselves be used by that cosmic Love, both as persons toward persons and in social groups toward social groups. In the Christian church we ought to see a spearhead of this movement of love in the world, so that not only "sympathy and understanding," such as the song asked for, but concrete love in action, will bring about increasing mutuality in every point and part and place. This is the Christian vocation in the world and without this social outreach all talk about personal "salvation" is likely to be empty or self-defeating.

But responsibility does not end there, either. We are related to the world of nature—to the very soil of the earth and to everything in the natural order which is our home and with which (as we have seen) we have an organic connection. In some of the liturgical formulae of the Eastern Orthodox Church man is spoken of as "the priest" who represents the natural order toward God, singing the praises that sticks and stones, trees and flowers, birds and beasts would sing if they had voices to do so. Here is a lovely symbol of human responsibility for the world of nature, to which we must respond if we are to live at all and for whose care we have a duty laid upon us. Do we use these things of the earth, such as natural resources, for the best good of our fellows and for the necessary conservation of these resources so that future generations may benefit? Do we truly respect the world of nature or do we regard it as simply there to be exploited by us for our immediate and selfish profit? In recent years, the appalling misuse of the natural order has been brought very vividly to our attention by many experts and popular writers. They tell us that we are destroying the possibility of life on this planet through our carelessness, indifference, and outright exploitation. We need to awaken to our genuine responsibility here. Unless we do so disaster will be upon us. But even if disaster did not threaten, the responsible man who is becoming a Christian ought to be aware of his obligation here.

The realm of animal life demands a similar sense of responsibility. "Blood sports," callous killing of wild life, painful slaughter of the beasts we use for food, and the like, all show a failure to recognize human obligations toward the animal world. This does not by any means require us to become vegetarians, although for some such a decision may seem right. It does demand, however, that (to give one example) the slaughter of livestock should be as merciful and painless as possible, as efficient as we can make it, and confined to supplying the necessities for living and not turned into a matter of useless, needless, and heartless murder for the sake of what is sometimes called "fun." Fun, indeed! The great Albert Schweitzer used to speak often about "reverence for life." Doubtless he carried this to absurd extremes, but his attitude was more profoundly human and humane, as well as Christian, than that of the callous "sportsman"—and what an odd word to describe one who makes up his own rules and has no regard for the prey save to catch and kill it!—who maims and murders simply to satisfy what to some of us appears nothing but adolescent blood lust.

In all these ways man is called to accept his responsibility for the world of nature and for what he does with it. If we properly fulfilled our human function to be "stewards of the earth," as someone has styled it, there would be enough food and drink for everybody. There would be available for all a share in the necessities of life and even in some of the so-called luxuries. Even with the enormous population increase, we are told by experts, this would still be the case. It is the condemnation of privileged people and privileged countries that they have failed to see this human responsibility. Furthermore, man "come of age" has knowledge and expertise to make the earth more fruitful, rather than to use his technical skill to destroy. It is in such situations that we can see God's will for us to act maturely, rather than to think that we can run to him to provide for ourselves and others what our own stupidity and cupidity have failed to provide.

There are so many related areas that one can mention but two or three. For example, mention of the enormous population increase reminds us that we now have the knowledge which enables us to control births and through the use of contraceptive devices or pills plan responsibly for the size of families. Despite recent Roman Catholic pronouncements on this subject, the great majority of people (including Roman Catholic layfolk) feel the need for this responsibility and for the diffusion of such knowledge in lands where it is most needed. Nor do there seem to be any signs of a lowering of moral standards by making such information available. In any event, as we have already noted, moral standards are only *moral* when they are freely chosen norms of human behavior. Coerced morality in this area, or anywhere else, is no morality at all but only servile obedience to arbitrarily imposed codes, lacking the element of freedom basic to proper moral decision.

There is also the treatment of illness and most recently the question of the prolongation of life. In respect to the latter, what about the person who is in what medical men call "a terminal condition" and who prefers not to continue living as a vegetable when all hope for genuine human survival is ended. I do not wish to make any judgment about this particular issue, surrounded as it is by so many delicate factors about which at present there is disagreement. Nonetheless, the horrible spectacle of persons simply kept alive, against their will, with no real human self-awareness left to them, must force us to face the question of responsibility here.

In these different ways and in so many others, the point is not that man is engaging in stealing from God prerogatives which belong only to him. The case is very different. It is a matter of God's granting us both the knowledge and the right to accept responsibility where it can be exercised; this has come to be through the long course of evolution. God plans it to be so; God wants men to become responsible agents who will do for themselves, but under the lure of his never failing love and always in his presence and by the power which he has supplied as part of the "common grace" in the world, what they can and should do. God desires that men shall be as mature as they can possibly be, to learn from their experience and to act upon what they know. Like any good parent he rejoices when this takes place; he is not jealous of supposed prerogatives that must be kept safely in his own hands. He wishes to share these with men, in his wisdom knowing that this is what we are here for.

That our decisions will often be shortsighted or wrong is obvious. That is part of the human situation as it now exists in the world. Yet God can handle even that. It is odd when those who claim they speak for God seem to assume that he is not wise enough or competent enough to look out for things. The doctrine of providence means, among other things, that God can and does "provide for" all such exigencies, even at cost of pain to himself.

Finally, men both respond to and have responsibility in the sight of God himself. Perhaps enough has been said about this already. Here we need only note that for the most part the response to God is made through the response to the created occasions in which he is present and through which he acts. Similarly, responsibility toward God is most often through the same occasions. Yet there is the immediacy of a relationship, however mediated it may be, with God himself. The abiding source of human and cosmic refreshment is there; the opportunity of comradeship is offered; and from time to time, especially in prayer and worship, God's human children have what traditional theology calls the awareness of his "attentive presence"—which is to say, the moments when God is known as God, an awareness which may come when men consciously turn their minds, hearts, and wills toward him in an "attention" directed to him alone.

What has been said in this chapter can be summed up in the language of the New Testament. We are creatures of God, made of the dust of the earth upon which the Spirit of God is breathed. God calls us to be his sons, delivered from slavery into "the glorious liberty of the children of God"; as sons, we are also called to be his friends and his fellow-workers. In Jesus Christ what is true about man in God's purpose is placarded before us in a new, vivid, and compelling way, but in him also we know the reality of God himself stated and expressed in human terms. He is "the image of the invisible God" as well as the pattern of human perfection into which we are intended to grow as we become men in him. From him there comes a strengthening in our sonship and an acceptance of us for what we may be, once Christ has been "formed in us." Commitment to Jesus Christ as both divine action and human fulfillment does not reduce our freedom, however, neither does it take away from our personal and social responsibility as men in community.

Through response to God's act in Christ—and to the degree that men have responded elsewhere to what God is always up to among them—there is "salvation." To be "saved" means to be made whole; the very Greek word *soteria* may be translated as health or wholeness. We are saved to wholeness *from* our limitations and from the deviations and distortions of our manhood; we are saved *to* a life which is lived in love which is identified with the "love of God that was in Christ Jesus our Lord" and hence is nothing other than being "in Christ." In our turn we are called to be "saviors," men for others because men for God; salvation is no escape from the world but a sending of men into the world to labor for God as the "fellow-workers" they are. To be "a man in Christ" is to be on the way to becoming a Christian. It is to be set free to love, not hate, to be courageous, not fearful, to be open, not closed in upon oneself. In this world, imperfect as it is, our loving will be tragically imperfect, but it will be genuine. The root of the matter is in us, so to say; the Christian may rejoice in this human privilege at the same time as he finds himself humbled by his human responsibility and shamed by his human failure.

As to the future, we may recall some words from the first letter of John: "Now are we the sons of God, and it does not yet appear what we shall be." The future is in God's hands, not ours; yet we have the confidence given by our present sonship. Nonetheless, the writer goes on to tell us that "we shall be like him"—like Christ, that is, since in us and through us God is working his good will, not only in spite of our recalcitrance but through our acts of free decision. He never allows men to be satisfied in their narrow and self-chosen ways but continually urges and invites them to venture out into broader ways and less selfish ones. There is a "more" which he sets before every one of us, to which we may respond. This "more" is the fulfilled reality of that "glorious liberty" which comes when in all freedom yet with complete responsibility his children say their "Yes" to his graciousness.

In this entire movement God is "prevenient," as theologians say, to our response. He comes before and invites us. He lures and attracts. He surrounds us with solicitations to find our joy in his service and he strengthens in us our desire to care for others. He will receive us finally into his own life, rejecting the evil we have done or finding some way to use it for a greater good, and accepting what good we may have accomplished and using that too.

With such a gospel, a Christian lives by faith in God and what God unfailingly provides. He lives in love, which can become more real to him and more adequately expressed by him. He lives with hope. The future is secure in God's hands since he is faithful and inexhaustible. God's love can never be defeated. His children can live consciously by that love, if they will. So they will become true men, which will be their dignity and their glory.

7

On the Road to Maturity

We have seen that man is "come of age" and must accept responsibility for what he does and for the world in which he does it. But we have also observed that Dietrich Bonhoeffer, when he used this now-familiar phrase, did not intend to suggest that man is now fully mature, "grown up" in the usual sense of the word. Yet he is most certainly on the way to such maturity; he is becoming what he has it in him to become. That is why this chapter is entitled "On the Road to Maturity"—on the road, but not yet entirely *there*.

But as we have insisted, the call to man is to continue moving in this direction. Paul spoke about the "full-grown man" as the goal toward which we are striving. We are no more babes, he said; we are men. Let us then act as men—and for Paul that meant assuming the full privileges as well as all the obligations attaching to those who are becoming "men in Christ." May I suggest, therefore, that Bonhoeffer was not saying anything very new. Paul had already said it; so have many other Christians. The difficulty has been that what Paul and others said was forgotten for a long time by many people; even the church itself tended for centuries to assume that its members were to be treated as children who must be told what to do and then forced to do it.

We who are Christians, the New Testament says in another place, are to "run the race" that has been set before us. We are to set our sights high, "looking unto Jesus, the pioneer and the completion of our faith," and we are to be content with nothing less than fulfillment as "sons of God." If we take these and other passages in the New Testament seriously, we shall be in no doubt about the vital quality of the Christian life and we shall know that to walk in the Christian Way is demanding of our courage and loyalty. In becoming mature men in Christ we shall be committed people.

There are many important aspects of the process of growth to maturity. It is impossible in a single chapter to look at all of them; hence we must choose one which is both interesting and relevant to our contemporary position as Christians in the making. The one that I have selected for our consideration is human sexuality. For younger Christians this aspect of growing to maturity is obviously central; it is not less central to older ones, although many of them are not so much aware of this central position. One of the purposes of our discussion will be to show just why it *is* central.

Surely the fact of human sexuality is undeniable. Its significance, however, is not always so plain to us. Young people realize this significance more readily than others, because they are vividly aware of the desires and drives of a sexual sort with which they are forced to reckon. Sometimes sexuality constitutes a problem for them. But I do not think that this is the correct way to come to terms with the matter. Human sexuality is no problem in itself; it is simply there; it is integral to manhood and must be accepted as a given fact in our experience. What we are to do with it is another matter; it is at this point that the problematical side comes to the fore. Thus the logical order of discussion should be first a consideration of the fact of human sexuality and then an attempt to look honestly at some of the questions which it raises. We must know the significance of sexual desires and drives before we can ask how best they may be expressed in concrete situations by men and women who are moving toward full manhood.

I have said that sexuality in itself is not a problem but a given fact. Yet it is tragically true that through a considerable portion of Christian history and even today in some quarters, the given fact is regarded with a large measure of dislike and distrust. There are reasons for this, in terms of historical development. In the very early days of the Christian church, the Greco-Roman world which was the setting for the faith in Christ was prepared to take a highly ambiguous attitude to sex. On the one hand, there were those who practiced, even if they did not defend, utterly licentious ways. Some of the great cities, like Corinth, were "sinks of iniquity," as the saying goes. You have only to read some of the contemporary literature to see that this was the case, while certain of these ancient writers produced vigorous attacks on the free and easy sexuality of the time. On the other hand, there was a type of thought which we know as gnosticism, that regarded the human body and its functions with horror and would much have preferred that men should be entirely spiritual beings. One great pagan philosopher, Plotinus, was said to be "ashamed of having a body" at all. The gnostic type of thinker was strong in his insistence on absolute control of bodily instincts and desires, sometimes to the point of demanding that those who were genuinely spiritual persons should abstain entirely from sexual activity.

Faced with this situation, the first Christian centuries were much more likely to adopt the second of these attitudes as more closely resembling the right measure of control that they believed necessary. They were horrified by what they saw in so many places in the Gréco-Roman world; in any event, they could not have accepted licentiousness as possible for Christian disciples. Their mistake was in confusing control with condemnation; they fell victim to the negative way of looking at sexuality found among the pagan gnostics. It is easy to find many instances of this negativity in the writings of early Christians. Despite a charge frequently made against him, Paul is not really guilty of this, although some of the things that he said could later be used by the people who distrusted the body and feared all sexual expression. The church never officially adopted gnostic ideas, however; we may be grateful that in principle it always held to the Jewish acceptance of sexuality as a good part of God's creation. Had there been any official acceptance of a view that had far too wide popular acceptance, the situation would have been very dark indeed. But largely because of the conviction that Jesus had been truly and fully a man, the church could not condemn the body; because in the sacraments, bread and wine and water were used, it could not condemn material things; and because the relation of God and men had been compared to human marriage, building here on Old Testament images and stories as well as on the beauty and wonder of Jewish-Christian family life in those days, sexuality could not be rejected altogether.

What did happen, however, was the establishment of what we may style a "set of mind." This looked upon marriage as a second-best. True Christians were urged to refrain from sexual activity, so far as possible. Toward the material world an attitude of condescending accommodation was adopted. Even in such wholesome Christian writers as Clement of Alexandria, the distrust of the body and of sexuality is obvious. When we come to Augustine, that enormously influential Christian thinker of a slightly later time, we may well be horrified by much that he has to say. In his youth, before conversion to his mother's faith, he had lived a licentious life—or so he said in later days, although in fact his behavior was not unlike that of most of his associates and certainly cannot be called strikingly loose or lustful. When he was converted to Christianity he "put away" the woman with whom he had been living in an arrangement which was by no means unusual at the time. He looked back on his preconversion days with horror. As time went on, his attitude toward sex became darker and darker. In certain of his writings, notably in some chapters of the great work of his last days, *The City of God*, he has extraordinary things to say. He believes that the evil in sexuality is in the urgent passion it involves. He speculates on how the race might have been propagated had men not fallen into sin and hence become victims of such passion. He supposes that it might have been possible to have some sort of sexual congress so rationally controlled that there was no excitation of the sexual members. He does recognize that sexual union is necessary if children are to be born into the world. But what we may call the pleasurable aspect of sexuality, with its physiological and psychological concomitants, was to him so dreadful that he wished it could be done away.

Augustine's influence and that of those who thought like him was great. When we couple with this the growth of monastic life, with its abjuring of marriage and its elevation of celibacy as a "higher" and a "better" state of life, we can readily see why it was that for a long period the whole sexual side of human experience was given unfavorable treatment by Christian theologians and moralists. Something of this spirit is still present in much that has been written against the use of contraception, as also in many discussions of problematical aspects of sexual behavior like premarital relations, not to mention such matters as homosexuality and (very much a matter of concern to Christian moralists for centuries) the almost universal practice of masturbation. The whole area of sexual life, in its many aspects, has been bedeviled by this sort of negativity, by distrust, and by fear. In devotional writing, in manuals for self-examination, and in many other ways, man's "lower nature" (as it came to be called) was regarded with horror.

It would not be a great exaggeration to say that only within the last one hundred years, perhaps the last fifty years, has a different and healthier attitude come to be generally accepted. Most of us today would reject altogether the negative position on human sexuality. We have returned to the ancient Jewish view that sexual drives and desires are part of God's good creation—hence, that sexuality is a good and not an evil part of man's existence. It is bad only when it is misused, like everything else in creation; and then it is not sex itself which is bad, but the wrong use of it.

In an earlier chapter it became clear that it is an error to think of ourselves as pure spirits or minds to which a body has been attached. We are not "angels," which in the definition used in the Middle Ages were called "disembodied pure intelligences." However, we are not just bodies, perhaps more complicated than other beasts but essentially nothing more. We are *persons*, which is to say that we are complex unities of body, spirit, mind, will, desire; all these together in one, and growing in integration as we mature. We also saw in that chapter that person and society belong together, so that a man without or apart from his fellowmen is less than a genuine moving toward selfhood, while a society in which all personality is lost is an ant heap, not the human community. Both of these truths need to be kept in mind when we discuss the significance of sexuality in human life.

Now if man is made to become a lover, so that he realizes what basically he *is*—however frustrated he may be in his expression of love and however distorted that expression may be—then *all* of man must be included in this thrust toward fulfillment. His spiritual yearning for mutual relationships in giving-and-receiving is part of the picture. So also is his emotional feeling which impels him in this same direction. Most of us would grant this, as we would also agree that the mind of man has its part in the selection of those who are loved. But not all have been ready to recognize that our physical nature—our biological aspect, our glands, and whatever else goes to make us up—is also to be included in the picture. It is the whole man who loves or wishes to love; it is the whole man who receives love from others. As he moves along his particular routing of experience and happening, all of man is involved. In the achievement of his selfhood it is the whole man who achieves. So also in his loving, it is the totality which is functioning. Furthermore, since man is set in community, his loving is inevitably and naturally with those of his own race, the race of men. He seeks relationship with another, finding in the mutuality there possible a fulfillment of his total self. He is helped toward that fulfillment by the ones whom he loves, as they are helped toward theirs.

There is nothing surprising about this. It is the way we are made and being made. It is to be accepted as an entirely natural fact about human life. Thus I insist once again that sexuality, which is the total fact (including body and mind, will and emotions, desires and drives, the physical members which we commonly call specifically sexual, and everything else) of man's drive for love in terms of its natural basis in man's organic stuff, is a given or a *datum* of humanity itself.

Beyond this, however, there is an even more important point to be stressed. We have said that man is made to become a personalized instrument of the cosmic Love, with whom he is intended to be in fellowship which deepens as life goes on. How could embodied creatures like ourselves come to grasp, and be grasped by, Love in that cosmic sense, unless it came about through the very embodiedness which constitutes our selfhood? This is why the wisdom of the Christian ages has always been prepared, in spite of its distrust of sexuality, to see that marriage is a symbol of the relationship between God and man. In what Luther called (speaking of the sacraments) the "in, with, and under" mediation of spirit through matter, we come to our meeting with God. We are brought to know the ultimate through our meeting with the proximate. This is the sacramental way of seeing things, deeply rooted in the whole biblical understanding of man's way of knowing the divine, although that rather abstract way of stating it is of course not found in the very concrete and practical language of scripture. The human drive toward fulfillment is "in God," in the Love which loves us and would have us become lovers. To make this possible for most of us, the drive finds its expression in human "falling in love," where boy and girl marry, desire and enjoy sexual contacts of a physical type, but through the whole experience find a mutual relationship which enriches both their lives.

Perhaps much if not all of what has now been said will seem obvious to the reader. Yet I feel that it had to be said within the context of Christian faith. This is because we must make crystal clear that no

Christian need be ashamed of his sexual desires. They are good in themselves and they are there to be enjoyed. The sexual experience, in its joy and in the anguish which often accompanies human love, is one of the best things in human existence; we can say boldly that God wants man to have pleasure in the sexual expression of his love. As the saying has it, "sex is fun"; it is meant to be that, although it would be unrealistic to forget the pain which is almost certainly present in the depths of human sexuality. Only those who have never known the experience could forget that. But only those who fail to grasp the beauty of sexuality could think of it as unpleasant, nasty, dirty, or see it only as a "duty" to engage in sexual relationships simply to propagate the race.

The procreation of offspring is the usual consequence of the sexual act, when this is engaged in between men and women. At one time it was taken to be the *purpose* of sex, but today most Christian theologians would say that the purpose is the mutual love and the sharing of life which the act both expresses and enhances. The procreation of children is a consequence of this sharing. It is as if the love of man and wife were so real and abundant that it overflowed into another life, indeed brought that other life into existence. The very word procreation is significant here too. Procreation: that is, man and wife create a new life as the agents of the God of love who is always creating new life everywhere in the world. It is the dignity of procreation in marriage that it reflects this divine fecundity, as we may phrase it; the human privilege is to be the instrument for this creation, so far as our race of men is concerned. The family circle, of husband and wife and children, is a little cell of love in the world, not to be narrowly hugged but to be generously shared. In that sense, as somebody once said, *every* family is patterned after "the holy family" into which Jesus was born and of which he was a member.

The problem posed by sexuality arises in connection with the question about how best it may be expressed. The long history of the human race shows that the way in which most people find a right and satisfying expression of their sexuality is through marriage and the establishment of a family. A man and a woman marry; they live together and share together; they have children for whom they care. Their physical sexual union is the outward manifestation of their inner union; it is also the way in which that union becomes more deeply personal.

There are other men and women, constituting (the experts tell us) about 5 percent of the population, at least in countries where studies have been made, who find themselves sexually attracted not to persons of the other sex but to members of their own. These are the "homosexuals"—a word, by the way, which is derived from Greek (*homo*) and Latin (*sexus*), meaning lovers of their own sex—whose numbers are larger than used to be thought and who are increasingly vocal in their claim for the rights and the recognition which for a long time they have been denied. This is not the place for any discussion of homosexuality. It is mentioned here only to indicate that for those who find themselves in that condition, it is not only inevitable but (at least in the judgment of many, including myself) morally right that they should love members of their own sex and desire contacts of a physical sort with those they love. Obviously this must be under control, just as the heterosexual's physical sexuality must be controlled. Considerable attention has been given this matter in recent years, not least in some of the great Christian churches. The result is a lessening of contempt and condemnation and the acceptance of the homosexual of either gender as a person to be respected and loved.

This is by the way, however. What I am urging here is that sexual expression in some fashion is natural and proper for human beings. Of course there are some few men and women who believe themselves called to a celibate life, without overt sexual contacts. In some Christian churches there are monks and nuns, vowed to this mode of life. There are also those who have felt so strongly the need to dedicate themselves to a given task that they are unwilling to marry. Some would wish to marry but for one reason for another cannot or do not; it is possible for them, with some effort, to deny themselves physical sexual activity. Yet in all these cases it is wrong to say, as some have done, that a "vocational" life without sexual acts is entirely *a*-sexual. Some years ago a Roman Catholic monk, Father Gerald Vann, wrote a fascinating essay in which he urged that what really happens (at least for monks and nuns—and I should add for others who conscientiously abjure physical sex) is the rechanneling of the sexual drive. Father Vann said that nobody can or should wish to *kill* his sexuality; this would be destructive of something utterly essential to human existence. But one can care for others, work for others, live for others, in such a fashion that the sexual drive is diverted into this activity. For most men and women, however, this is so difficult that it is nearly impossible, save by that special divine help which Christians would call the grace of God. Most people not only wish to have an expression for their sexual nature; they need to have it, lest they become warped and twisted personalities, who do not go forward in wholesome human becoming but tend to be bitter, jaundiced, even downright nasty in attitude. The phenomenon known as the "spinster" is a manifestation of this; oddly enough, the male sex is more likely to produce the "spinster" than the female.

There is a tendency both to overvalue and to undervalue the physical expression of human sexuality. It may be overvalued in that it comes to be regarded as the only thing in life that matters. Some of us may have known people of this sort. They are obsessed by sex; they seem unable to see anything save from a sexual angle; they are always seeking opportunities, good or bad, for having sexual contacts. The tragedy here is that such persons lack all proportion in their lives. Every aspect of human existence should be understood and accepted in its proper place and time. Man *is* a sexual being; but he is not able to "spend all his life in bed," as someone has put it. It is also the case that in the first flush of discovery of the wonder of sexual experience, young people tend to overvalue its place in the totality of their growth toward maturity. This is no matter for surprise; most of them learn, soon enough, to have the necessary sense of proportion. An older person of this type, however, does not present a very pleasant spectacle to his associates or friends.

It is also possible to undervalue physical sexual expression. It may be seen as an irrelevance and its implementation in practice regarded as necessary only to satisfy one's partner, or to fulfill one's marital "duty," or to produce offspring. But such undervaluation can be as disastrous as overvaluation. The man or woman who purposefully tramples on his sexual desire is likely to end up in that state of "spinsterhood," with a warped attitude toward human sexual love, to which we have referred. Those who seek to kill their sexuality, with its physical manifestation in some form, are all too often twisted characters with no spontaneity or openness in their relations with others; they are always afraid that "sex may raise its ugly head" in such relations.

The title of this chapter was "On the Road to Maturity." I believe that human sexuality is a powerful factor in helping human beings move forward on that road. By such intimate physical contact and union, men and women are helped to realize their significance as lovers in the making. In a wholesomely balanced human life, moving forward toward true manhood, sexual activity provides an opportunity for the development of those qualities which are part of loving: self-commitment, mutuality, trust, hopefulness about others, giving and receiving. The anguish which sexual existence can bring assists in the deepening of emotion and the recognition that there is an inescapable element of the tragic in human existence too.

In Genesis, we read that God saw that "it was not good for man to be alone"; so God provided for man a "helpmeet." God established the possibility of a community of love, in which his human children might come to know what it means to be in deepest relationship one with another. The story makes an important point that needs always to be remembered. We are "members one of another," by virtue of being human; sexual love is a sign and symbol of this truth, not to be dismissed as irrelevant and not to be made the only thing in life.

Some may think that talk like this is merely sentimental. I cannot agree. It seems very shortsighted to dismiss the "romantic glow" which is found in human sexuality so frequently and often so disappointingly. Those who reject all "romance" are making far too sharp a distinction between agape, self-giving love, and eros, love that yearns for a response. They are taking far too light a view of the place of passion in human growth. In fact they show themselves inhuman. There are few more suitable symbols for the divine Love, which ever seeks union with his creatures, than the joy and delight— and the strange pain too—which a boy and a girl feel in each other's company when they are in love. Nor can there be any symbol more appropriate for the divine Love than that which is found in scripture: the sexual relationship of lover and beloved. It is no accident that the Jewish and Christian traditions have seen in The Song of Solomon, that highly erotic bit of Hebrew writing which got placed in the Old Testament, a profound symbol for the love between God and man or between Christ and his people.

Yet in all sexuality there is need for control. Uncontrolled sexual expression is more like the barnyard than like true human community. Others must be respected; they must be treated as what they are, men and women moving toward true manhood; they must not be coerced; they must never be "used" by another simply as a means for physical gratification. In love all satisfaction is *mutual,* because love means and is relationship or sharing. William Morris once wrote that "fellowship is heaven and lack of fellowship is hell." How true this is! When there is no control, fellowship in the deepest sense is lacking. If "hell" is the place where the only word heard is "I, I, I" (as an American poet has said), then sexuality which is entirely self-regarding is very close to hell; there is no fellowship in such sexual expression.

But what kind of control do we have in view? In recent years there has been much talk of "permissiveness." If this means the opening of possibilities for sexual expression without any control whatsoever, the result will be disastrous. But if one may add to the word permissiveness two others which I have heard spoken by some young people of my acquaintance, things will be different. These words are "affection" and "responsibility." The former is a synonym for love; the latter has to do with that awareness of human obligation about which we spoke in a preceding chapter. In that case, we can look at each of the three words and see how control may properly be exercised in sexual life.

"Permissiveness" would mean in that context that society did not seek to smother or refuse the expression of sexuality because this or that particular mode of expression was unusual or unpopular among conventionally minded people. It would see that sex cannot be "legislated" into the right paths; only by free decision can human beings show themselves to be truly moral. "Affection" would mean that sexual contacts are always to be grounded in a genuine love between the persons involved. Thus "commercial sex" or "occasional sex" would be condemned, not by outraged moralists but by lovers themselves; the latter know very well that the deep satisfaction of the whole person comes from such a total union of lives as love makes possible. In that situation, physical sexual acts have their place as expressive of true mutuality. Finally, "responsibility" would mean that nobody would "use" another person as a means to his own relief or pleasure, as if that other were but a tool convenient to be used when and as we wish with no regard for the other's feelings, desires, and needs.

In essence, this suggests that the truest and best sort of control is what we might style "love-control." It is control, not by one's own wishes but by awareness of the other person. The result may be the working out of a code (if that is the right word) of sexual behavior which is different from, but not necessarily worse than, the one which has been conventional. One of the great needs of the moment is the working out of just such a code. Young people today are beginning to see this. They are far less promiscuous than their elders often think; they are also far more honest than an older generation could claim to be.*

I have written in criticism of Augustine's jaundiced attitude to human sexuality. Now I must note that in one respect at least the great African Christian theologian of the fourth and fifth centuries was very wise. He spoke of the way in which sexual life is a manifestation of the depths of human personality—to him those "depths" were very dark indeed, hence sin and sex were closely associated. For us, believing that the "depths" of man are grounded in the ongoing Love which is God at work in the world, a more positive attitude is possible. Human sexuality reveals *both* the glory and wonder of love in action in the world *and also* the ever-present possibility (and sadly apparent fact too) of distortion and frustration in loving. Thus we may conclude this chapter by repeating that in human sexual love we see how man is being made into, is becoming, the personalized instrument of the divine or cosmic Love. And we see also how deficient man is and how easily he can take the wrong path in that movement toward his true manhood. Both sides are there; neither can be overlooked.

* It is a pity that only a few outstanding Christian writers on moral issues have been prepared to assist in the working out of such a code; we may be thankful, however, for those who in recent years have dared to interest themselves in such matters. Here I am thinking particularly of one essay—it seems to me the most perceptive and useful of the many I have read—written by Paul Lehmann in a recent book called *Sexual Ethics and Christian Responsibility*. It is impossible here to summarize Lehmann's argument, but the main conclusion is the necessity for "joining freedom with responsibility in sexual experience and practice" (*Sexual Ethics and Christian Responsibility*, ed. John C. Wynn [Philadelphia: Westminster Press, 1970], p. 57), and there are suggestions of some ways in which this may be done.

8

Praying and Worshiping

I have spoken frequently—some may think too often—of man's "coming to be," his becoming that which is intended for him. I have also spoken about the place which his own free decisions must occupy in this process of becoming a true man. There is no escape from such decision-making. But it must not lead anyone to assume that this means that man is entirely "on his own" and that by his own efforts he is able to make actual the potentialities which are his. A doctrine of "self-help" which made such a claim would be more than absurd; it would be a contradiction of the facts of the case.

No Christian could have thought otherwise. When Paul tells us that we are "to work out our salvation with fear and trembling," he adds at once that "it is God that worketh in us." The relationship between human effort and divine assistance is not easy to state, but both sides must be kept before us. It is by God's gracious favor, working through and with the response that we make, that our "salvation" is brought about. Christians know that they can never earn, through hard work or through good deeds, the fullness of life which is promised to them in Jesus Christ. It is always "of grace"—that is, it is a gift. But they know also that they must do their utmost in responding to what God does for them and in them; they cannot excuse themselves from that kind of effort.

Quite apart from Christian faith, however, the approach to the significance of human existence which has been taken in this book would make any idea of the sort impossible. For we do not live in a world where every man is "on his own" and where he can, of himself and by himself and for himself, come to the true manhood which is his goal. On the contrary, the world in its processive and societal nature demands cooperation, participation, and sharing. Nobody and nothing exists in isolation from the rest of the creation; everything, without exception, is in relationships and lives from and by these. Thus a sound view of how things go in the world precludes the notion of advance through individualistic effort alone. We have dared to say, too, that *God* is in relationship. He does not depend for his existence on the creation and what happens there. But for his concrete and actual nature as Love-in-action, he is influenced and affected by that happening. He cares for his world; and to care for anything is to be open to its action upon one. God's transcendence, we have seen, is not his remoteness or his self-containedness but his faithfulness, his resourcefulness, his inexhaustibility, each of these exceeding human comprehension.

In filling out this picture, Christian faith brings to vivid focus this point about relationships. For man is not only in never-ceasing contact with his environment in all its aspects; he is also in a give-and-take relationship with God himself. God's self-giving love is placarded before us in Jesus Christ. It is also "shed abroad" through that same Christ, as men come into contact with him, find themselves lured to and grasped by his continuing action, and discover that their truest existence is "in Christ"—"in Love" which is available to them in their own human terms because brought near in a Man. Thus genuine human love, as we know it and live it when we are true to our deepest selves, is the reaction to and reflection of the divine Lover. Or, in words from the Russian novelist Tolstoi, "Where love is, there God is." The English recusant poet Robert Southwell phrased this in a beautiful sentence: "Not where I breathe, but where I love, I live."

A Christian sees the truth of these sayings. And any man, who has pondered at all deeply the meaning of his own existence, also has a glimpse of how deeply sayings like this penetrate into the very heart of the matter.

We have observed that the difficulty with our becoming the lovers we are meant to be arises from frustrations which are beyond our control, but more seriously from our own accumulated decisions which have distorted and disordered our capacity to love. For this reason Augustine could say, in another of his moments of insight, that what was needed was "the ordering of our loves." Man's deepest need is to have his loving, the objects of that loving, and the ways in which he loves, rightly *ordered*. He needs to have his capacity for and desire to love given the proper pattern. Only so can he move toward his real fulfillment.

It is at this point that what Christians call "the grace of God" becomes crucial. God's grace is not to be understood as something extraneous to God himself; it is nothing less than God in his loving action upon men. It is not a "thing" which is poured into us. Despite the words of an ancient prayer, which speaks of God's "pouring his grace" upon us, the truth is that grace is much more a personal relationship, to be interpreted always after the analogy of those relationships which we know one with another in ordinary human experience. We might even define God's grace as his personal and personalizing relationship with his children in utter loving concern. If this conception of grace had always prevailed in Christian thinking, a host of problems would have been avoided—for example, the ancient dilemma of God's grace and man's freedom. Does not grace deny true freedom of decision? Does not the human capacity to choose freely deny or remove man's need for grace? The answer to these questions is hard to find if we think of grace as coercion or as a thing brought to bear upon us. But once we have seen grace in terms of the definition just given, we can grasp the way in which grace fulfills human freedom. Far from free decision-making grace unnecessary, it is precisely *in* our freedom that we receive grace. The human lover knows very well that between himself and the one he loves there is no problem as to who gives what; it is a matter of gracious mutuality and sharing, in which each gives to the other, each becomes one with the other, each plays his full part in the life of the other. The integrity of each partner is retained completely, yet the two are so much at one that there are no absolutely distinct separating boundaries between them.

The lover always finds his freedom in experiencing the self-giving of the one he loves, for self-giving does not remove the requirement for response freely made and joyfully received. "Your wish is my command," we say. By this we mean that with a sense of complete freedom, our response is made; the point of the freedom is in the making of the response. Thus we can use quite properly traditional words like those which speak of God's "service as perfect freedom"; or we can see the truth in George Matheson's hymn, "Make me a captive, Lord, / And *then* I shall be free." If this is a paradox, let it be one; as so often in human experience and thought, we must say two things which are not contradictory but complementary. Another one of Augustine's remarkable insights is found when, in writing about exactly this question of God's gracious activity and man's required response, he adds, "Only he who loves will understand what I am saying." The lover understands the truth of the paradox; and since all men are being made lovers, if they will let it happen to them, they all catch some glimpse of the truth.

Our discussion has brought us to the place where we can begin to think meaningfully of prayer and worship. When these factors or elements in Christian discipleship are separated from the context which has just been provided, any discussion of them is abstract or speculative. Prayer and worship have their setting in a vividly felt relationship of God and man, where grace or love-in-action is coupled with human response in returning love. In prayer and worship we have the opportunity for a consciously sought and attentively open relationship. Thus prayer and worship are not in some peculiarly unworldly sense intended only for very "spiritual" people. They are part of a whole movement of God toward his creation and of the creation toward God. One of the significant developments in recent years has been the recognition that this is the case; this explains so much that has been written about what are called "new" ways of engaging in prayer and participating in worship. As a matter of fact, the great masters have always known what is now being rediscovered; the sad thing is that so many were neither taught nor helped to see it.

Nonetheless, it is true that the conventional ways of praying and worshiping make little sense to many today. This is why we must welcome the work of those who are trying to find new approaches to the subject. A little book like Pierre Teilhard de Chardin's *The Divine Milieu* is worth its weight in gold, because it puts prayer in the context of a world in process. Suggestions for prayer like those of the Abbé Quoist in his *Prayers* are invaluable because they relate the exercise to the concrete experience of men and women in the contemporary world. Robert Raines, the American Methodist minister, has given us several admirable little books which provide a method of "meditation" that makes sense to us where we live today. As to worship, men like Bishop John Robinson in his *Liturgy Comes to Life*, not to mention others like Boone Porter, John West, Massey Shepherd, and Ernest Southcott, have made it possible for us to engage in public congregational worship without feeling that by doing so we have withdrawn from the world and engaged in an impossible (and incredible) attempt to fly up to the heavens.

Our concern in this chapter, however, is not with such details, important as they are. We are interested in the point or significance of engaging in prayer and worship. Once that point becomes clear, questions of method or techniques can then become meaningful and helpful. So we must first attempt a definition of prayer, in the personal sense in which each may engage in it for himself; after that, we shall say something about public worship, in which a group of Christian people join to support and help each other in becoming that to which they are called, responding in community to the loving action of God.

It is unfortunate that many people, even instructed Christians, seem to think of prayer as an attempt to bring to God's attention what otherwise he would not know or to coerce him, by subtle means, to grant to them something of which they feel a need or desire. The reasons for this mistake are many. One of them, certainly, is the notion that prayer consists only in petition and intercession. These are important parts of prayer, but when taken out of context they can become dangerous, leading to the idea that the exercise of prayer itself consists solely in "asking." When seen in the proper context, however, they are anything but the magic which tries to discover formulae to get one's way in the world. As to the matter of telling God what he does not yet know, the absurdity is apparent; prayer is not an exchange of information but a union of persons in close and intimate relationship, as we shall see.

The best definition of prayer known to me is this: prayer is the aligning of our desires and yearnings with the great cosmic desire or yearning for good which is God himself. If we spell this out a little, we can understand that the very essence of prayer, in Christian practice at least, is the intentional and attentive identification of our feeble human willing, purposing, and aspiring, with God's enormous loving care and activity. The person who prays is seeking above all to let himself be used by God in his self-giving, so that this person may become more fully the personalized channel for that love at work in the affairs of the world. When Jesus said, in the Garden of Gethsemane, "Not my will, but thine, be done," his words expressed the very heart of this prayerful identification of deep personal desire with the purpose of God.

There is a possibility that we shall misunderstand the purport of those words of Jesus, however. Some have taken them to mean a passive acquiescence, as if the stress were to be put in this way: "Not my will, but thine be done, bad as it is, unwilling as I am to find it agreeable to me, but nonetheless to be accepted without murmuring." This would be a slavish submission to whatever may happen with the assumption that of necessity this will be God's will. But Jesus did not pray, any more than he lived, in that fashion. His words should be stressed so that they mean, "Not my will but *thine be done*." There is a positive, affirmative, active quality about these words when they are repeated with that emphasis. It is as if Jesus said, "Let me be utterly identified with God's loving purposes and used by him as the instrument through whom they are to be accomplished."

God's will is his purpose of love-in-action, for the widest possible sharing of good in the world and for the continuing creation of more occasions of good. My will is limited to what I see in my small way to be desirable; it fails to reach the ever-widening perspective of God's perfect love. Perhaps now and again I can include in my willing the good of others but I have only a very slight grasp of the sweep of the divine purpose. In prayer I seek so to open myself that my imperfect, limited, and defective willing may be brought more closely into accord with God's unfailing and cosmic purpose of love. And I pray that God's will for good may *be done*, for prayer is primarily prospective, a concern for what can happen in the future, although that can include also penitence for what in the past has prevented me from serving the divine purpose as I might have served it. In prayer I ask that I, unimportant as I am and with my limitations and defects, may still be used for the doing of good in the world. Thus Jesus prayed that God's will should be done through the awful destiny of arrest, trial, crucifixion, and death that awaited him—he urgently desired that through his suffering and dying the divine Lover would achieve a purpose which would be for the bringing of men into right relationships with their heavenly Father.

When the Abbé Henri Bremond spoke of prayer as "the disinfecting of self," he was making much the same point. But one could wish that he had not referred to "self" in what seems a pejorative way. The better phrasing would have referred to the "lower," imperfect, limited, narrow self, with which our better self—urged to move toward fulfillment—may often be in conflict. For it would be quite mistaken to think that in prayer, or in any other aspect of human experience, we should wish to destroy ourselves, although most certainly we should wish to purify our motives, widen our vision, correct our mistaken perspective, and remove the danger of continuing defect and deviation in our yearnings and desires.

It is a common human experience to find that when we identify ourselves with some good cause or person, we are delivered from a too self-centered concern and made free to act boldly and gladly on behalf of whatever-it-is which has commanded our loyalty. This is a valuable analogy for understanding prayer. By the aligning of our desires with God's purpose, by the identification of our will with his, we may be freed from immediate self-concern for interests and objects that are of the sort to interfere with our truly becoming the selves which we know to be for our best fulfillment—and this, be it remembered, always in community with our fellows.

At the heart of prayer, interpreted in this fashion, is a rejoicing in the sheer goodness and love of God, with thanksgiving for all that we receive "from his hands," and with a renewed dedication to his service. Inevitably this will lead to a recognition of our own failings, defects, and distortions of the possible or actual good. Only then can we make sense of petition and intercession. In any event, these are not to be taken as demands made upon God for what seem to us desirable objects. They are the honest bringing into his consciously realized presence, of the persons, causes, needs, which we cannot fail to recall before him but of which he (of course) is already well aware. Prayer as intercession or as petition is not a magical formula to obtain our desires; it is an inevitable "recollection" of all that we think we or others need in order to fulfill God's purpose in the world. Our vision is so partial, our grasp so weak, our understanding so inadequate, that what we bring before God in this manner will hardly be what we *really* want, deep down underneath our superficial thinking and feeling. Many things that we think or feel we need are not for our best good at all; prayer is a way in which our sense of these needs is purified. We have no occasion for fearing that we shall be condemned if we speak simply and honestly about such matters; God understands. If we are prepared to grow in prayer and are open to the pressures of the divine Love upon us, we can begin just where we are, in the confidence that a similar growth in response to that love will come, sooner or later.

The divine wisdom is so all-encompassing that it may always be trusted. God knows what has happened and what is happening. He knows also the relevant possibilities in the future, although because he respects the freedom of his creatures he cannot and does not know exactly which of those possibilities they will choose before they have actually made their decisions. Furthermore, since his love is faithful and subtle, he can be trusted to bring good out of apparent evil, where this evil happens, and "make even the wrath of man turn to his praise." Paul has a passage which in correct translation it is very important to remember: "In every respect God works toward a good end for those who love him." As a child comes to have utter confidence in a loving parent, as a workman comes to trust the foreman who knows his business, as a student comes to trust his teacher when the latter has proven his competence in his subject and his interest in the ones whom he teaches—so men come to trust God, who most surely knows what he is doing in the world and who is possessed of adequate resources to accomplish this, as he also desires only the best for each and every created entity.

There are obstacles in the way, both for God and for men. These are summed up when we use the traditional words "evil" and "sin." If there are obstacles, due to recalcitrance, distortions, deviations, frustrations, backwaters, drags, or (to use Teilhard's word) "diminishments," there is also a battle against them. Good strives to overcome evil, love hate, beauty ugliness. In a world that is still being made and with men in process of becoming their true selves, this is to be expected. We may conclude that a world like that is a better world than one in which everything is a finished product and there is no freedom with the consequent likelihood of error. The Christian faith is the assurance that the evil *is* being overcome, the good *is* being realized, hate *is* being defeated, love *is* winning the victory. That is the hope in the Christian proclamation. Prayer is human identification or self-alignment with God as he works in *that* way. It makes it possible for men to be consciously "fellow-workers" with him.

We turn now to a consideration of public worship. We need not spend so much time on this subject, since we have already prepared for it by what has been said about prayer. Public worship is the corporate praying of the Christian fellowship and obviously much that applies to personal prayer is applicable to it. But it is important to make one point, a point that is increasingly realized today by Christians of all denominations and backgrounds. *The* act of worship which is centrally and distinctively Christian is the Lord's Supper, the Holy Communion, the Eucharist, the Mass—call it what you will, according to the tradition in which you have been brought up or which you now find attractive to you. The reasons for this centrality are obvious.

The Lord's Supper had its origin in the table meals which Jesus and his disciples shared, chiefly in the "Last Supper" on the night before his betrayal and arrest. Throughout the history of the Christian fellowship of believers it has always been the heart of their worship, for through participation in it and above all in receiving the bread and wine which Jesus called (at that last meal together) his "body and blood," they have felt themselves most intimately in communion with him. There have been many different theological interpretations of the meaning of this sacrament, in which material things become the instrument for a personal relationship of the Lord with his faithful people. But these interpretations are not so important as the realized fact of his presence and the awareness of his love and power brought to bear upon the lives of those who participate.

The action of the Lord's Supper—for it *is* an action, something done as Christ is believed to have "commanded and taught," in words from an old liturgy—is two-fold or two-way. First there is God's giving of the presence of his Son Jesus Christ to those who receive the sacrament. In doing that God is in truth giving *himself*, since the reality of Jesus' life was the activity (hence, as we now see from our grasp of the processive nature of the world, the *presence*) of God in the manhood which was born of Mary. Thus the first movement or direction of the Eucharist is toward man, in that here is God's superabundant love poured out through a Man for those who are made one with him. But second, there is the offering or dedication of the Christian believers who are present. In this service they are glad to offer themselves, souls and bodies, life and work, to God as he is made known in Christ. Their prayer is that God will accept what they seek to offer, will bless it and use it, and thus will bring those who offer themselves into the circle of his continuing loving action in the world.

The symbolic way in which this is done is instructive. Bread and wine, things of the earth which have been "processed" and made into the food and drink necessary for man's sustenance, are taken and set apart. They are offered to God for his use, along with the lives of those who have brought them. And then, in Christian belief, they are returned to men by God, blessed and given a new meaning. For now they are the instrumentality through which God gives us his life in the life of his Son Jesus Christ. When a sermon is preached at the celebration of the Supper, as it ought always to be, it proclaims the gospel which asserts just this fact that the sacramental action enacts in a concrete way. The love of God for men, declared in Jesus Christ, evokes the response of commitment so that those who are present may become, what by God's intention all men are being made to become, lovers of their fellows and channels of the divine Love.

Frequent attendance at this sacrament, where possible, has proved itself through Christian history as a chief, if not *the* chief, way of making real the significance of Christian profession and bringing those who call themselves by the Christian name a step farther on the Christian Way. Even when one does not *feel*, in some emotional sense, the deep significance of what is going on, Christians nonetheless should try to attend frequently. We all need to remember that God is greater than our feelings and that his gift of himself in Christ is granted even when we are not vividly and with any great intensity aware of what is going on.

We have noted that almost all Christian denominations are now stressing the importance of this mode of worship. They are seeking new ways of making it meaningful in the contemporary world, since many of the older forms under which it has been observed tend to obscure its real significance. This is not to blame our ancestors in the faith, who surely did the best they could do about these forms. But we have a better grasp of the background of the Lord's Supper in Judaism, a greater awareness of its historical development, and (we may dare say) a deeper appreciation of the way in which it both symbolizes and expresses the reality of Christian discipleship. Thomas Aquinas once said that "in this sacrament the whole of our redemption is comprehended." With that judgment both Protestants and Catholics now agree.

There are other types of worship, familiar to us all. Simple morning and evening services, in which the sermon is central; musical services, where God is approached through the beauty of harmony; special occasions for teaching those who come to learn—we need not go through the list. The point to be stressed is that precisely because man is a societal being and above all because Christianity is a fellowship, we cannot "forsake the gathering of ourselves together" in a public acknowledgment of God and in a common strengthening of our lives to walk in the Christian Way as we move forward in becoming true men, lovers in Christ.

I end this chapter by repeating what was said at the beginning. Prayer and worship are utterly integral to the Christian life of discipleship. However we pray, through whatever means and by whatever methods, pray we must. And public worship, chiefly in the Lord's Supper, is not only a privilege for Christians but should be seen by them as an obligation or duty. We need the help of others in our Christian life—but above all we need what I have styled the attentive and intentional consciousness of the presence, power, and love of God which worship and prayer make available to us.

9

Looking Toward "the End"

Earlier in this book, we told the story about Schopenhauer and the policeman who asked him who he was and what he was doing, with Schopenhauer's answer, "I would to God I knew." The policeman might well have asked still another question, "Where are you going?" —and to it he might have received the same response.

There can be no doubt that one of the questions which most men and women, at some time in their lives, ask with a terrible urgency and often with poignant anxiety, is just that. "Where am I going?" "What is my destiny?" We want to have some assurance about who we are and what we are here for. But we also wish to glimpse something of what awaits us. We look toward "the end"—the end of our mortal life here on this planet and we wonder if that is indeed *the* end. Perhaps we have never heard the New Testament word *eschaton*, "the last thing"; but the "eschatological" problem, as New Testament scholars call it, is always with us. If we have some sort of answer to the first two questions, about our identity and our vocation or responsibility as men, we need also to have an idea of what is the *ultimate* conclusion of the matter. Identity, purpose, and destiny go together.

We have argued that man is on the way to becoming truly human, a lover who is a strangely complex body-mind organism, with rationality, will, and emotion. We have said that his purpose or significance is found in his becoming the personalized instrument for the cosmic Love which we call by the personal name God. In this chapter we shall think about human destiny. As we go forward in our pilgrimage, walking in the Christian Way, what is "the end" toward which we may look? Is it simply a matter of this present life, comprising at best ninety to a hundred years? Or is there something more for us?

Two possible answers suggest themselves immediately. The first is the response which would be given by the materialistic thinker who believes that, since man is only a collection of particles of matter or energy, he is going *nowhere*. His existence lasts for a few years on this earth; then comes death—and that is all. I recall a little incident which was instructive to me. A medical doctor was talking to a group of theological students about the advances which science has made in the treatment of disease and the prolongation of human life. Then he added, "But do not forget, gentlemen, that despite all this the death-rate remains at precisely 100 percent." Of course he was speaking the truth; it is important that we do not forget it. The man or woman who has not honestly faced the fact that within a few years, at best, he will die, has not yet come to terms either with himself or with the world where he now lives. Not that we should brood over our coming death; that would be absurd and unhealthy. We should *recognize* its coming, however, and we should see that the certainty of death lends a poignant quality to everything that we do and to everything that happens to us.

The doctor whom I have quoted was not a materialist; he did not think that death meant the "end" in the sense of the absolute conclusion of the matter: "this is it, there isn't any more." But not a few people would say just that. And to say it and live as if it were true is one possible way of answering the question of human destiny. The answer is that there is *no* destiny for man.

But there is another possible answer. We die, of course; that is the fact. But is that all that can be said about our "end"? For a long time people have said that this is not the case at all. They have said that while our body dies, *we* do not die; and by this they have often meant that there is something about us which they call our "soul" which is immortal and which bodily death does not affect in the least. They talk like the familiar American song, "John Brown's body lies a-mouldering in the grave / But his *soul* goes marching on." The soul of man is taken to be indestructible; hence man, in that part of him which is his *real* self according to this view, is by nature indestructible too.

This position runs into many difficulties. If man is a complex body-mind organism, if his existence as man is exactly in such a complex organism, how can a soul or mind exist without the body in which it dwells or of which it is an aspect? The French philosopher Gabriel Marcel has told us, as have others, that it is a mistake to think that there is an *I* who "has a body"; the truth is different from that. Man *is* a body, just as he is also a mind or spirit. Our identity is in that rich complexity, not in some abstract "spirit" which abides eternally. So much are our bodies and the relationships in which they exist integral to our selves; so much are we tied up with and exist in the embodiedness which is ours and which makes possible all our contacts and brings to us the material about which we may come to think and will and feel—that it is difficult to see how our identity could be preserved if the body were simply sloughed off.

For a Christian, the notion of soul as this view holds it presents difficulties too. The ancient Jews and the early Christians, as their scriptures make clear, did not talk about "the immortality of the soul." That was a Hellenistic idea which certainly invaded some late Jewish and much Christian thinking; but it is not the main line of biblical teaching. Later Judaism and early Christianity talked about something quite different, "the resurrection of the body." This too presents many problems, as we shall see; but we ought not to confuse the biblical affirmation of resurrection with the Greek idea of immortality.

I should reject the materialistic view that death is the end of everything. But I should also reject the doctrine that the "soul" of man is immortal and indestructible, and hence persists after death in some ethereal heavenly state. Neither view seems to me to be true and neither makes much sense when I begin to look at myself here and now. On the one hand, I have a sense of "bright shoots of everlastingness," as a poet put it, which permeate and give light to my mundane existence. I have some kind of "intimation," as still another poet said, of a *more* that moves in and through the world and through my own life. So I cannot think that physical death is the absolute end, especially when I take into consideration the truth of experience upon which we have been so insistent. I find myself in my capacity to give and to receive love; somehow, in that loving which is possible for me and which now and again I know in all its wonder, there is a hint of an eternal quality over which death has no power. When the lover says to his beloved, "I love you now and to eternity," he is saying something that has real meaning, even if we find it hard to put that meaning in clear and precise words.

However, I do not know anything about a "soul" which is supposed to be the real *me*. What I do know, in this present existence of mine, is the total body-mind organism which is myself, with its complex association of desires and yearnings, strivings and seekings, thinking and willing. I feel myself to be this sort of unity; and I can never say whether my body or my mind, my emotions or my will, are doing or receiving; all I can say is that the self which is a total entity is doing the things *I* do and receiving the things *I* receive.

I reject both these possible answers, then. But if I reject them, what is there left to say about human destiny, about "the end"? The question could be phrased in this way: Granted that I am this whole and total entity, this identifiable routing of experiences and happenings, how can I think of an end, a final affect of everything, including myself, which is not just finis—"full-stop," with the story entirely over and done with?

In the attempt which will now be made to arrive at an answer to *that* question, we must be very careful and very attentive. What I shall suggest may not be easy to grasp, especially if it comes to the reader as a very new idea. Since most talk about a *more* has conventionally been in terms of "soul" with its presumed indestructibility and immortality, another sort of view may be misunderstood. For this reason, I must ask the reader to follow the discussion as carefully and attentively as possible, for I do not wish to be misunderstood, nor do I wish to appear to deprive him of a belief which is very dear to him. I do wish to urge a way in which his belief in something more than mortal existence can be put on a firmer basis, in the light of the conceptuality of process and love which has been central to our whole argument in this book. What will be said will come under two headings: the question and the hope.

We turn first to what I have styled "the question."

In posing this question, some preliminary remarks must be made so that the issue may be seen in its proper setting. We have talked a great deal about God as sharing in his world's happenings and as affected and influenced by what goes on in it. We have said that the good which is accomplished is received into God, for his own delight but also for use in the further development of his purpose of shared love. The evil in the world he cannot receive in this fashion, since it is the contradiction of his nature of love; yet he *can* overrule it by extracting the possibilities it provides for deeper, subtler, more harmonious good. Of this, we have noted, Jesus' death on Calvary when coupled as it must be with his triumph on Easter Day, is for the Christian the great paradigm or model. But irremediable evil, if there is any such, God can only reject. Thus from our perspective we can say that God knows intimately and immediately everything that is good; he has accepted it and received it, he enjoys it and he uses it. The evil he must know *as evil*, even on those occasions when he has overruled it for good ends. In a word used in the Bible, God "remembers" what has happened, the good as good, wherever and whenever it has been achieved; likewise he "remembers" the evil which has happened, although this he does not take into his ongoing relational life.

What is here indicated is that something is everlastingly preserved, despite what Whitehead called "the perishing of occasions." The good which has been achieved abides forever in God's "memory"; the evil does not do this, but God is yet always aware of its having existed and he has extracted from it whatever good he *could* receive and use.

And now for the question which has to do with us men who are agents of the good, although alas! we are also agents of the evil. Can the good which has been accomplished through our free decisions, which God willingly recognizes, *really* be preserved if the agents who have been instrumental in accomplishing it do not also continue in God's remembrance forever? We are not speaking here of "souls"; we are speaking of human personality as a whole and in the making. As it happens, the Jews seem to have meant just this total personality in the making when they spoke of the "resurrection of the body." That phrase was their way, under their own circumstances and in their familiar patterns of thought, of indicating the whole man. The "body" was for them man's historical existence in all its complexity yet in all its growing unity. It must not be confused with "flesh and blood," at least in the later and more developed strands of Judaism and in early Christian thought; Paul himself makes that very clear when he says that "flesh and blood cannot inherit the kingdom of heaven."

This, then, is my question. Is it conceivable that God can value and preserve, keep and remember, enjoy and use, the many goods which he has worked with his human children to bring about—good acts and thoughts, truly beautiful and admirable achievements of all sorts in the created order—unless he also values and preserves, keeps and remembers, enjoys and uses us through whom these goods have been achieved? My answer to that question is that *in some way* God must do just this with us. I am frank to say that I do not know *how* God can do this. I can draw no precise map of "life beyond death"; nor can anyone else. Yet because God is love, the cosmic Love, he must cherish forever what is worth cherishing. I am permitted to trust that in doing this, he will also cherish my dear friend or that loved person who has been the agent for accomplishing this good.

That leads us to go on to speak of the *hope*, the other aspect of the matter.

Let me emphasize that it is hope about which we are speaking, not some kind of absolute certainty which is open to no doubt. In the *Book of Common Prayer* there is a fine phrase: "a holy and religious hope." That gives us exactly the right attitude to the matter. If we talked about utter certainty, we should be dishonest for we do not possess the knowledge which would be necessary for this and it is wrong to speak as if we did. One of the things that most horrifies outsiders is the way in which some Christians seem to assume that they have everything "laid on the line," so that there are no uncertainties in their faith. To talk in that fashion, I believe, is to deny the very nature of faith itself. As Paul Tillich used to urge, the distinctive thing about faith in the Christian sense is that it is sure commitment held in the face of whatever evidence there may be to the contrary. It is "courage," as he liked to put it—the courage to make just such a commitment even when much would seem to argue against it. Much does argue against the Christian hope; if we hold to it, we must do so in the face of that contradictory material and not pretend that everything is entirely plain and that there are no difficulties or problems.

Now it is worth noting that belief in personal existence after death is not a necessary corollary of faith in God. For most of their early history, the Jewish people believed most firmly in God but they did not accept any notion of personal survival of death. They thought of some vague existence which they called "Sheol" where the shadows of the dead persisted; but Sheol was a terrible place where "the dead praise not God" and where tenuous survival meant nothing at all save the inability of the Jew to think of absolute annihilation. Wiser Jews said very little about this, in fact. Doubtless it was not important to them. Only in the period of the Maccabees did the teaching about "resurrection of the body" come into prominence. This was on the grounds that God would surely not fail to reward or punish those who had participated in one way or another in the Jewish struggle for freedom from alien and pagan rulers. God's righteousness demanded that he vindicate those who had supported the Jewish battle for survival as a people and that he punish those who had failed to support it.

The specifically Christian affirmation of life beyond death came from the conviction that Jesus Christ had been "raised from the dead" and that those who were "in him," united with him in communion and fellowship, would share in his rising and would live in and with him forever. Furthermore, the disclosure of God through Christ as utterly loving played its part in the development of this doctrine. How could a God who had so lovingly created and continued so lovingly to provide for his human children permit them to pass out of his presence because they must suffer death? Could he not secure their abiding life with him, not so much as a reward for their achievements as a gift of his free grace? The motivation in each instance was pure and right. But there has always been a danger, and there still is if one listens to some people speak about the subject, that this conception will be turned into a "glory for me" view. A selfishly individualistic notion of life beyond death, in which man tries to play dog-in-the-manger to the universe, has nothing to be said for it. Christians who know what they are saying will speak rather of a "communion of saints," a beloved community of men and women in God, in which those who have shared in such love here and now will be participant in it forever. The Christian hope, when it is properly grounded, can talk only in that way; this is what a Christian, as one who is becoming what he is called to be, may hope for.

Such hope is not a wistful thought that maybe things will turn out for the best. It is an eager, earnest, and joyful expectation—"tip-toe expectancy," as Baron Friedrich von Hügel used to say—that in some fashion, about which we have no clear notion, God will guarantee to all who are "in Christ" a share in his kingdom of light and life and love. Even those who do not knowingly speak of Christ, or who have not met him "in the flesh," may very well be *in* him if they have served his cause of love and have been caught up into the divine Charity which it was his mission to reveal.

What has been said may seem cold comfort to those who expected some ringing affirmation about heavenly bliss promised to them if they were loyal Christians. I am forced to say that I think that people who expect such assurances are mistaken as to where the emphasis ought to be laid in this matter of human destiny or "the end." We have spoken of those who seem intent upon playing dog-in-the-manger to the universe—and to God. They seem to say that unless they are guaranteed their own little piece of glory they cannot endure thinking of God's triumph over evil, hatred, and wrong. But surely such an attitude ought to be impossible for a Christian. The ancient maxim says *ad maiorem gloriam dei*—"to the greater glory of God." That is what should be emphasized. Everything is to *God's* glory, not to ours.

What then is God's "glory"? It cannot be selfish satisfaction on the part of deity, since God is not in the least like that. He is sheer self-giving Love who delights in receiving the response of love from those whom he is luring to fulfill their existence as true men who are being created to become lovers in the making. God's glory is nothing other than the ever wider and more inclusive sharing of his love, as he works in his world to conform everything to the pattern of its possible perfection. In that case, my own deepest satisfaction will be in contributing to that glory—which is to say, in doing everything in my power to make the regnancy of love apparent, while my greatest delight will be in his using me toward the achievement of his purpose. Whether or not I myself happen to be aware of how this is being done is a very secondary matter. It is not a trivial or unimportant matter, to be sure; but it cannot have the first place in my thinking as one who is becoming a Christian. Faith is commitment to God's love in Christ in spite of everything and it includes a readiness to give myself to God for whatever destiny or "end" he has in view.

Yet, as we have argued, God's greater glory is not the denial of the good of his children. Being what he is, he wants and is able to preserve all the good which human life has accomplished—and our hope is that he will also preserve the agent who has been instrumental in this accomplishment. For the agent, precisely insofar as he has been instrumental for good, is himself also a good and is worthy of God's unfailing remembrance.

The discussion up to this point may have seemed to have a certain ambiguity. On the one hand, we have been intent on the preservation of good in God; on the other, we have had the hope, but not the absolute certainty, that this preservation will include the human agents of good. At the same time, we have admitted that we have no information about how God may do this. Hence I am in the position of saying that I should not dare to claim the necessity of my own personal survival after death. Yet I should claim, *for God*, the readiness and capacity to "keep that which has been committed unto him." If this means that, in the words of the psalmist, "I shall see of the travail of my soul and be satisfied" when "I wake up after his likeness"— well and good. That is my great hope. It is not a hope for myself alone, however. It is a confident expectation about *God* and it is inclusive of my human brethren, whoever they may be. This is theocentric, as theologians say; it is focused on God. It is also outward looking, for it never forgets the brethren, with whom I am so much involved by virtue of my being a man, a person in social relationships.

All that is said about human destiny or the "end" is also said about the here and now of our life. This is why in John's Gospel and in the letters attributed to the same writer in the New Testament, the words "eternal life" occur so often. As they are used in that literature, they do not have to do with the unending prolongation of this earthly existence in a postmortal one. That may indeed be the case; but the writer is speaking of a quality of life, a mode of human existence, which can be known and shared in this present moment. "This is eternal life," we are told, "that they may know thee, the one true God, and Jesus Christ whom thou hast sent." Not by postponement to some later time, but in the "now" in which we live, eternal life is offered to men if they will make response to him. Eternal life is the present abiding in the love and life and light which the Johannine writer tells us is central in God. To share now in this life is to have the "earnest" or "first-fruits" of our destiny or "end"; we do not need to wait until some remote future. To participate in God's purpose, to be caught up into his outgoing love, to be grasped by his self-giving, to find ourselves most truly "in love" and hence "in Love." This *is* eternal life.

Once we recognize this, we can also see that there is a present significance in what traditional theology has styled "the last things." Our *death*, which is bound to come; *judgment or appraisal*, by which our contribution to the creative advance of love will be evaluated; *hell*, as the absence of fellowship and the self-centered refusal to care; and *heaven*, as the fulfillment of our becoming in true manhood, as those who have learned to love—these all have immediate relevance for us now, whatever may be said about them in respect to the future.

The fact that we all must die makes us aware of the necessity for the readiness to die daily to our narrower, more self-centered, less open and generous selves, so that we may live in outgoing concern for others. We face daily appraisal as to the way in which we are becoming true men as lovers. As St. John of the Cross, the Spanish poet and mystic, wrote, "At the evening of our day, we shall be judged by our loving." That "evening" is but the culmination of the judgments or appraisals which day by day indicate the degree of our growth and the quality of our concern. If we refuse fellowship with others and attempt to insulate ourselves against their influence, taking the center of the stage and proudly thinking ourselves "monarchs of all we survey," we experience the barren wastes of hell. But if we live for others, sharing in the common life, participating in love with them in their concerns, we know the joy of heaven.

Through it all, the central motif is the divine Love which is "sole sovereign lord." Thus we are brought back to the clue to the meaning of our existence. The clue is love—we have repeated this time and again. Yet it cannot be repeated too frequently, for we are all prone to forget it in the rush and bustle of daily life. Let us say once more that the love about which we are talking is neither sentimentality nor cheap romanticism; it is the obdurate, astringent, and purifying love which is ready to go to any lengths for the loved one. It is the love which was unveiled for us on the hill of Calvary. It is this love which makes all the difference between a purposeless, futile, sterile, and inane existence, such as we might well find ourselves forced to endure, and a purposeful, significant, fruitful, and intensely meaningful life, intended for us by God as his children move on toward full manhood and become ever more truly his sons.

If Christian preachers and teachers and theologians had put their stress there, but of course without the imperfections and mistakes that I have made in writing about it, how much deeper would have been our Christian understanding! How much more adequately would we all have come to see what becoming a Christian means! And how many theological puzzles and problems might have been avoided, difficulties which to a considerable degree have been occasioned by a readiness to make some other, less basically Christian concept the criterion for Christian thinking. Above all, we might have been delivered from those "faithless fears and worldly anxieties," of which the American *Book of Common Prayer* speaks. "Perfect love casts out fear," John says. So, learning the centrality of love, we might have lived more bravely and more sincerely as Christian disciples.

If we have learned nothing else from the events of the last century, from our renewed appreciation of biblical thought, from contemporary philosophical ideas, from the new perspective in theological study, we have learned at least this: that love *is* central in Christianity and that only when faith is stated and lived in such a way that its centrality is evident, can it make any sense to ourselves or to our hungry, needy, weary, and yearning contemporaries. Such a love is inclusive of the tragedy of life. It plumbs the depths of human anguish; it knows the heights of human joy. It is *God's* love and God *as* Love. This is the gospel declared in the event of Christ; this is the faith which responds to him; and this is what Christianity is all about.

10

Helps to Discipleship

It is now time to sum up the argument of this book and state its conclusions. After that I shall make some suggestions of practical helps to Christian discipleship, ways in which our becoming Christians may be strengthened as we continue walking in the Christian Way.

To put it briefly, I have urged that nobody has the right to think of himself as already a Christian; everybody must recognize that Christianity is a movement or advance. In some words from William Law, we may speak of the "process of Christ," by which he meant the reproduction in the faithful believer of that which Christ himself experienced. In doing this, we are going forward along the path which Christ blazed for his followers and on which he still accompanies them as a refreshing presence. We went on to say that, in thus becoming Christians, we are members of a fellowship with its roots in the past; we did not invent the Christian faith for ourselves but were incorporated into a community which lived by it and which sought to implement it in the affairs of the world. This meant, we said, that there is an abiding Christian stance, from which we start and which we can never forget. Love is the secret meaning, now disclosed, of the mystery of the world and of human experience; the purpose of our life is to grow in that love and learn to express it in as many places and as many ways as may be open to us.

But today there are some special difficulties about all this. We mentioned three of them which seem to be particularly important: the way in which we make our model of God; the special place we give to Christ; and the significance of the non-Christian religions. As to the first, our contention was that only when God is seen as nothing other than "pure unbounded love," and all other ideas of him are secondary to this, can we give Christian faith a genuine significance. In respect to the second, we noted that the special place belonging to Christ is found in his focusing at a point, and thus disclosing vividly, the universal activity of God as he works ceaselessly in the world. Christ is not the supreme anomaly but the classical instance. He is our clue to everything else, not separated from everything else which may have brought a glimpse of the divine reality to men. This led us to say that the non-Christian religions cannot be dismissed as unspeakable errors; they should be seen as partial intimations of the divine character and as places where God has indeed worked savingly for his children. The decisive quality of Christ, known to Christian faith, is not to be denied; but his "uniqueness," to use the common word for this decisiveness, is inclusive of all that is true and good and God-given, not exclusive and self-contained.

Then we observed that there are two significant factors in much modern thinking which can play their part in assisting us to grasp Christian faith today. These are the concept of evolution or process in the world, leading us to see that nothing here continues in a fixed condition but everything is moving forward toward some end or goal; and the stress on the absolute importance of love as the deepest truth about how things are going in that creation. The former helps us to see how God is intimately related to a world of change and himself is influenced and affected by the process of the world—far from being a static and inert first cause or unmoved mover or substance or absolutely fixed omnipotent will, he is involved in and shares with his world, enjoying enriched experience through that which happens and using such happening to augment the further expression of himself. And he himself is indeed love, for love is always in such relationship and rejoices in it as also it suffers with it.

Our next chapters dealt with man's own nature as a "becoming." He is on the way to true manhood, which means that he is on the way to becoming a lover who can serve as the personalized instrument for the divine Love and in thus serving find his own deepest satisfaction. Alas, through wrong decisions which have led to distortion and deviation, the choice of the good is difficult; we have tried to reckon with the facts of evil and sin, although we have refused to give them the last word. *God* must have that last word; his victory as cosmic Lover is the assurance of faith. Responding to him, as men are intended to do, they are given responsibility as "come of age," to take upon themselves the obligations and share in the privileges which God wishes for them. To try to evade such responsibility is to deny true manhood. But our manhood is not complete; we are "on the road to maturity." In proceeding along that road, we have seen, the sexuality which is so integral to us has its very significant role to play. Man's sexual desire and drive provides the condition for his realizing the meaning of love; and in relationships of a sexual sort with his fellows he finds a surrogate or agency through which he may come to know what love toward God may signify.

Finally, in the last two chapters, we spoke of prayer and worship and the role they can play in bringing us along the road to fulfillment; and then of "the end" or human destiny, in which finite men are given a share in the divine life through God's "remembering them for good"—remembering that which through them has been achieved in the creation and also, as we hope, remembering the agents through whom the achievement has been wrought with God's continual gracious help, in the common affairs of life as well as in the particular and special ways in which he makes himself known to us in his own personal integrity as companion and refreshment.

Throughout this discussion, I have tried to be honest. Most of us have little use for somebody who talks as he is supposed to talk but fails to say what actually he thinks, deep down inside, to be the case. In any event, since God *is* truth we do him no real service when we fail in speaking what to us seems the truth. Nor do we commend Christian faith to others when we speak with less than complete candor about our own convictions, admitting honestly the problems or difficulties we face and acknowledging with equal honesty that we make no claim to possessing all the answers. It is my hope that readers have showed a similar openness, candor, and honesty. We have been engaged in an exploration undertaken together; it has not been my wish to impose ideas upon anyone, but rather to suggest points which are worth considering and which may be helpful to others who are walking in the Christian Way.

Now we may turn to our further suggestions. It is my belief that there are certain things which a Christian disciple may do, things which will prove of enormous help to him as he continues in becoming a Christian man. It will soon be seen that these things are quite simple; they may even seem conventional and familiar. But that does not mean that they lack value. In this instance, as so often, modern people may well profit by listening to their ancestors who have discovered that there are certain practices that have unfailingly helped *them*. Why should they not prove also to be of help to *us?* It is certain, however, that the value of such helps to Christian discipleship will depend largely upon the degree to which any one of us adapts them to his own use. There is nothing to be said for an idea that has been far too prevalent in some Christian circles: that people can be steam-rollered, so to say, or (to change the image) that they can be forced into some procrustean bed whether it fits them or not. Individualism is a mistake, but recognition of personal qualities, with diverse tastes and capacities, is a necessity if Christians are to be allowed to grow in their manhood with all the freshness, originality, and distinctiveness that will make their growth specifically their own.

I have said that my suggestions will be simple. That recalls an Old Testament story about a leper who made a long journey to visit a prophet so that he might be healed. The prophet told him to wash in a nearby small stream; and the distinguished statesman was annoyed. After all, there were great rivers back home and this prophet made such a tiny recommendation! I have discovered during my life that often enough it is the simple, not to say obvious, things that are most worth doing and that prove most effective. Perhaps that is because men are really themselves more simple than they like to think. Simple practices may be appropriate to them.

However this may be, here are five suggestions as to ways in which through regular disciplined practice we may be assisted in developing our Christian belonging and progressing along the Christian Way. They are listed first; comment on each will follow in due course: (1) Continued reading, study, and thinking about Christian faith, its significance and its application; (2) the setting aside of part of each day for reading the stories about Jesus and other New Testament material, with occasional reference to the Old Testament and to other writing that has to do with the origins and early development of the Christian enterprise, as well as the specific characteristics of Christianity; (3) a resolution to be regular in attendance at the public worship of some Christian church and especially to attend the Holy Communion frequently; (4) the giving of some period of time daily to thinking carefully and prayerfully in the attentive presence of God, opening oneself intentionally to a deepened relationship with the cosmic Love and putting oneself in the way of becoming more fully the personalized instrument for that Love—which we have seen to be the purpose for which we exist; (5) the decision to do some work, to act in some special way, for the assistance of other persons or for causes which promise to contribute to the wider spread of love, understanding, sympathy, justice, and goodness in the world; and along with this, the determination to support by money, letters, personal participation, or other means the organizations which have aims such as these.

1. When I speak of continuing one's reading, study, and thinking, I am not advocating indoctrination. I am suggesting that there is a great need for *informed* Christians, those who are prepared to use their minds in the service of Christ as well as serve him with their wills and seek his presence in their lives. In an age when more and more men and women are given the privilege of advanced education, it is essential that the Christian community be able to speak to them, while at the same time the Christian himself should be able to know enough about the faith he holds and the Way in which he walks to give some reason for his loyalty.

Reading of the Bible can be a mechanical exercise which does little good. It can also be a very enriching one, provided the reader takes the pains to read intelligently, carefully, according to plan, and with the use of the available guides and commentaries. There is no reason to assume that any portion of the Bible, opened at random, will at once make sense to us. After all, the books of which it is composed were written at different times, by different people, against different backgrounds, and with different purposes; the Bible is not all of a piece, although its main thrust is most certainly unitary. It is the story of God's fellowship with a given people, one segment of mankind, and it tells how through experiences of the most varied sorts that people came to know his character and purpose. Then in the New Testament it goes on with the story of Christ, given by those who had heard the oral traditions about him and who based their whole lives on his renewed presence and power. If the Old Testament is read, by Christians, in the light of the New—thus following Luther's suggestion that the point of scripture is that "it draws us to Christ"—the whole long tale can have enormous meaning. And the use of guides and commentaries is invaluable. Many are now available, not least the superb, many-volumed *The Interpreter's Bible*.

But our thoughtful and careful reading should not only include the Bible. Other material can be included; many lists of this sort can be had from various denominational educational boards and there are excellent bibliographies in such volumes as the recent Penguin *History of Christianity*. The reader who wishes to pursue such a course of study might even venture to ask his local minister! After all, one of the jobs of a clergyman is to assist others in becoming better informed about the Christian faith.

The purpose of such reading and study, it may be urged, is not inspiration. That is right enough and important enough; but what is so much needed today is information about how Christianity took its rise, how it developed, and (perhaps most useful) how it has adjusted itself to the problems posed by succeeding centuries. In this way, the man or woman who is intent on becoming a Christian *today* can trace the manner in which *in other days* people became Christian, brought their witness to bear, and were enabled to continue loyally in the Christian Way. We need not, indeed we cannot, imitate their particular responses; but we can make a "proportionate interpretation," as it was called by B. F. Westcott, and see how in our time too a response may be made to the initiating love of God in Christ.

Finally, under this heading, there is a need to acquaint oneself with the big issues of the day as Christianity bears upon them: war, race, class, national interest, international cooperation versus belligerent claims to local sovereignty, and the rest. The point here is not to say that there is *a* Christian answer to each of these problems; it is only to urge that a Christian should try to inform himself about the best contemporary Christian thinking on such matters. All this, taken together, can seem an enormous program. But ought we to expect that serving God with our minds is an easy and undemanding affair? If we think our commitment worth making, we ought also to see that it is worth intellectual effort, to the degree that each of us is capable of such effort.

2. We have already encroached on our second point while discussing the first. But now our interest is not in the reading of the Bible as an intellectual exercise but as what in an older day was called a "devotional" one, as well as the reading of other literature which will serve the same purpose. But we ought not to think, as some still do, that it is possible to make a sharp demarcation between the two ways of reading. We need to understand that a proper use of the

scriptures or other books for the deepening of our Christian discipleship requires us to use our minds. Yet there is a difference in intention which cannot be denied.

I may read the gospel narratives about Jesus' healing of the sick with the primary purpose of coming to grips with whatever of genuine history there is in these stories, with the resultant impact of Jesus as he was remembered, and with the way in which the healings had their place when the first Christians began to interpret their Lord as one "who went about doing good and healing all manner of disease, for God was with him." I can also read the same material in order to put myself in the place of the sick person whom Jesus comforted and healed. I can think of myself as the one who needs his strengthening love and concern, even if my illness is not physical but is only a defective will, a cold heart, and a less than complete commitment to him. Reading in this way, the words of Jesus addressed to that man or woman in Palestine can come alive in my own experience as if they were addressed to me: "Be of good cheer," "Take up your bed and walk," "Have faith in God." Much the same can be said about great works of Christian devotion like *Theologica Germanica, Imitation of Christ, Pilgrim's Progress,* and many others including such modern books as those of Teilhard, Quoist, and Raines, mentioned in an earlier chapter. I can read these to inform myself about how Christians have in fact thought about their discipleship at various times and places. But I can also read them so that I am helped to make their teaching and concern my own, as I continue on my path toward becoming a Christian.

I believe it is important here again to speak of the reading of the Old and New Testaments with the use of guides and up-to-date commentaries. These help to put the material in the right context; they also provide valuable suggestions as to the meaning of that material which otherwise might escape us. Knowledge of the facts will help us to the faith which thought the facts worth setting down. A reading of the Gospels, in particular, with attention to what experts have said (in *The Interpreter's Bible* exegesis and exposition, for example) can bring the one who reads to share the earliest (and the continuing) Christian insistence that in the Man whose remembered doings and sayings are found there, God had indeed acted with singular intensity to disclose his character and purpose and to make available his empowering Spirit of love. And that can bring us to a better knowledge of ourselves as professing Christians, showing us both the problems we must face and the grace which God will provide for us in facing them.

3. I have made reference to the words "Neglect not the gathering of yourselves together," found in the New Testament letter to the Hebrews. The writer was urging his readers to see that they did not fail to participate in the worship of the Christian community. He knew, like all the other early Christians, that nobody can be an individualistic Christian, seeking to "go it alone" in his discipleship and in his walking the Way. So it is for us today. We need others and they need us. That is one of the major reasons for including in our list the faithful attendance at public worship. There is another reason, even more important, to which we shall come in a moment. As to the Lord's Supper or Holy Communion, the centrality of this sacramental act of worship is more and more recognized; regularity of attendance at this service, with the reception of "the spiritual food of the body and blood of Christ," as both the Anglican and Methodist service books put it, is the highest privilege the Christian knows. Other kinds of worship are not lacking in value of course. But this one is utterly decisive. We have already seen why this is the case; our response to its decisive nature in Christian public worship should be regularity in attendance at it.

In participating in worship we are helping others as they are helping us. But we do not attend such services in order to enjoy ourselves, although we may now and again (perhaps to our surprise) find that we are actually "having a good time." The basic motivation is the need a Christian feels to do what an old saying calls "giving God the glory." *That* is what public worship is all about; that is its basic purpose. Not that we should imagine that God "enjoys" being endlessly serenaded by his children! That idea would put the truth in a false light. Rather, God so much cares for his human children that he wishes them to experience the self-cleansing and invigoration which come when they stop thinking about themselves and do something because it is good to do—and "giving God the glory" *is* good to do.

When that motive is central, then the corporate witness borne by Christian people as they gather together is entirely proper as a consequence. We share and we give. Participation means this. We also receive and benefit, since participation brings this too. Nor can we forget that each of us has his own idiosyncrasies, his own quirks and twists; we profit when we are with others who can fill out places where our experience is lacking and correct those where it is narrow and limited. R. H. Tawney, the distinguished English economist who happened also to be a devout Christian, once wrote some telling words: "If a man seeks God in isolation from his fellows, he will find not God but the devil; and the devil will bear a surprising resemblance to his own countenance."

We need not deny that the way in which public worship is sometimes conducted, often by a well-meaning clergyman, can be boring. So also some of the hymns and anthems may be sentimental or unrealistic. The sermon may seem irrelevant. Other members of the congregation may impress us as uninteresting people. What does all this matter? Once we have grasped the big point of public worship, we can put up with a great deal—and it may even be the case that the simple fact of "being bored" can do us good. Somebody once remarked that there was much to be said for boredom as a way in which a man's character was strengthened in the face of the unexciting aspects and moments of life. Yet public worship today is more and more well-conducted, with music and words that make sense to us, while ministers are being trained to preach sermons which are directly related to the practice of the Christian life and not exercises in theological speculation or expressions of personal ministerial prejudice. These ministers should have our support.

In the Holy Communion, however, such obstacles cannot loom large. For the point of that service is plain enough in terms of the actions performed, the material elements of bread and wine which are used, and the common reception of those elements by the communicants. It speaks for itself. Whether it be celebrated with great splendor, as in some Christian churches, or with equally great simplicity, as in others, it is unmistakable in its significance. This constitutes still another reason for frequent attendance at it.

4. The chapter in which we discussed prayer should have made its necessity in Christian life apparent to the reader. There can be no doubt that prayer is a much neglected aspect of that life, however. Some recent surveys indicated that among those who professed Christian allegiance, a considerable number admitted that they hardly ever prayed, although they were ready to think that prayer was a valuable exercise for such as practiced it. I believe that one reason for this

failure in prayer is simply that the way in which people have been led to think of it, as well as many of the traditional techniques of prayer which are still taught to "beginners," make little or no sense today. Our purpose here is not to discuss this question, but we can at least indicate that it may very well be the case that for our contemporaries prayer must be much more spontaneous, arising out of given situations and in the context of particular problems or issues, than it sometimes has been. Furthermore, it may be the case that such prayer as people find possible to engage in with heart and soul will be brief, pointed, and more of the type traditionally called "arrow prayers" than long periods of time spent in the address to God. ("Arrow prayers," for those to whom the term is not familiar, are simply short exclamatory phrases such as "God help me," "May I see how to face this issue," "Thank you, God, for this moment of joy," or possibly a few words of scripture, especially from the psalms, which seem appropriate to particular occasions in one's daily round.)

Nonetheless, some of us are sure that there is still place for a period of time daily, when, for five or ten minutes, the man becoming a Christian opens himself consciously to the reality of God's presence, seeks to align his desires and will with the divine Love and its designs for good in the world, and thinks in God's presence of the needs of others as well as of his own needs.

Human beings are creatures of space and time and unless they make space and find time for this "attentive presence of God," as we have styled it, they are likely to be without much awareness of that presence in the ordinary situations of life. The particular time and place do not matter much. Some find very early morning a good time and their own bedroom a good place. Others prefer a short period before retiring for the night. Still others find it helpful to drop into a church and sit or kneel there for a short time. It does not seem to make much difference; each person must choose for himself—and in the hurly-burly of modern life it is sometimes not easy to find either time or place when one can be quiet in God's remembered presence. Yet one can try to find them. Those who care enough to try will usually succeed in this respect.

Whatever may be the words we use, or the absence of words if we prefer to let our thoughts turn to God without verbalizing them, it will be good if we end our prayer with a slow and thoughtful repetition of the Lord's Prayer and a simple commitment of our future days into the care of the cosmic Lover. All discipleship and growth in the "becoming" which is our calling is summed up in that prayer which Jesus taught his first followers: that God is to be adored because he is our loving Father, his will to be done by us, his kingdom established in us as the reign of love, our needs to be remembered, our defects forgiven as we forgive others, and ourselves delivered from fears and anxieties. Thus in us and through us the Spirit of Love which is the Spirit of God in Jesus Christ may be expressed, enacted, and extended.

5. The last suggestion in our list may be mentioned briefly. This is the actual *doing* of Christians, as they work at their discipleship. People often think that "Christian work" is assisting as an usher at church services, teaching in Sunday school, serving on congregational committees, assisting in campaigns for the financial support of the church. These have their place, of course; somebody has got to do these things. But Christian activity in the full sense is the doing of one's job in a spirit of loving awareness; it is the expression in concrete deed of concern for others; it is "visiting the fatherless and widows in their affliction," as the letter of James puts it. It is writing a letter to a lonely person, participating in some organization whose purpose is justice or peace, anything and everything that makes for a world where God's sovereign rule of love is more effectively at work. Perhaps in our own day it shows itself chiefly in support for movements that promise a better and happier world for all men, in the political, economic, national, and international spheres.

But what is here said generally must be done specifically. It is easy to "talk big" and then "act little." This is why the suggestion has been made that every day, in some fashion, a Christian should find one thing to do which will implement in concrete practice these generalities which make for good. The choice must be made by the Christian himself, whose free decision so to act is what counts most. Whatever may be decided as *this* day's specific responsibility, let it be done with a glad spirit, not as an oppressive duty. It is a *privilege* to be on the path toward becoming a Christian; our action should be a joyous expression of our sense of privilege, just as it should also be a faithful obedience to the will of God as we keep our eyes open and use our heads to find opportunities to practice in our lives what we believe in our hearts.